THE LEGAL WRITER

Third Edition

MARK P. PAINTER

in association with

JARNDYCE & JARNDYCE PRESS

CINCINNATI BOOK PUBLISHING

IN ASSOCIATION WITH

JARNDYCE & JARNDYCE PRESS

CINCINNATI BOOK PUBLISHING

©2005 by Mark P. Painter. All rights reserved.
Cartoons ©Marc Tyler Nobleman,
www.mtncartoons.com, used by permission
Design by Eberhard + Eberhard
Printed by John S. Swift Co., Inc.
Printed in the United States of America
Third Edition, April 2005

ISBN 0-9721916-8-2

The first edition of this book was dedicated to Walter Kobalka, Ohio Supreme Court Reporter, and his staff, who, by editing my decisions for many years, have taught me much about writing. Walter has now retired and is missed.

The next edition was dedicated to my appellate law clerks, past and present—

Steve Walker, Doug Dennis, Dave Back, Tricia Hackleman, Paula Welker, Richard Schaen, Phil Stephens, and Kathy Carter. I can now add Mike Majba and Mike Cappel.

They have shared the journey in writing for the last ten years. My assistant, Gail Ruth, has helped us all.

This third edition is dedicated to Christopher Dietz, the chief of staff at our court, who has been editing my work for more than ten years.

www.judgepainter.org

Contents

Acknowledgments

This is a revised and expanded third edition. The first edition was published in June 2002. It sold out fairly quickly. That gave me the opportunity to add a couple thoughts and examples to the second edition. The second edition also sold out more quickly than expected. This third edition is published in cooperation with Casemaker Print Publishing[R].

This edition is much less Ohio-specific. But I have continued to use Ohio examples, as these come more readily to my attention.

My affair with plain-language legal writing began when I attended a seminar given by Bryan Garner in 1995. It was a revelation. Not that my writing was awful before that and great now, but I understood so much more about written communication.

At our court, we have an editor who pores over every opinion. I strive to receive as few corrections as possible, but I have never gotten a perfect score. Christopher Dietz was also kind enough to review this work on his own time, and I appreciate his comments and corrections. Any errors are, of course, mine.

My wife, Sue Ann Painter, also read the work before publication. She was able to offer insights from a different perspective—she is a historian and fundraising professional who puts out a lot of prose herself. Sue Ann also helped with the production process.

Tony Brunsman, of Cincinnati Book Publishing, handled marketing—and did so well that the first and second editions sold out more quickly than expected.

Mark Eberhard, of Eberhard+Eberhard, designed the covers and formatted the text. He produced so many good covers that we had trouble narrowing down the choice. We finally decided to go with the one that communicates the most clearly. The cover on this edition is just slightly changed from the original. Mark has been a great help throughout my career.

**"Wish I could help, but I only
speak English and legalese."**

The minute you read something and you can't understand it, you can almost be sure it was drawn up by a lawyer. Then if you give it to another lawyer and he don't know just what it means, why then you can be sure it was drawn up by a lawyer.

Will Rogers

How We Got into this Mess

Some legal writing texts begin by explaining how legal writing is *different* from other writing. But it should not be. While certain documents—complaints, briefs, deeds—may have a standard *form*, their content should be in plain English.

Most legal writing is atrocious. Fred Rodell, Dean of Yale Law School before most of us were born, had it right when he said, "There are two things wrong with most legal writing. One is style. The other is content." This was in a fascinating article, *Goodbye to Law Reviews*,[1] which should be assigned reading for all law students. If you haven't read that article, I commend it to you.

---

1. (1936), 23 Va.L.Rev. 38.

Where did we learn to write? Grammar school is certainly not that any more; but we learned rudimentary rules in grade school. Unfortunately, some of those "rules" were not rules at all. The grade-school teacher who told you not to start a sentence with *and* really meant not to write "I have a dog. And a cat. And a parakeet." Those are not sentences. So the "rule" was just shorthand for making us write in complete sentences. The trouble is that no one disabused us of this notion later. As I will discuss later, the use of *and* and *but* to begin a sentence is one mark of good writing.

You can, but not often, split an infinitive. "To boldly go where no one has gone before" would not read or sound the same without the infinitive split. And you can end a sentence with a preposition when necessary. Winston Churchill: "That is a rule up with which I shall not put."

Some of us honed our writing skills in high school and college. We learned from reading examples of good literature and other forms of writing—from journalistic to persuasive. Unless we fell victim to academic-jargon illiteracy (a subject for a separate treatise), we usually got better with practice. Though we may still have been handicapped by some false rules from grade school, some of us became at least passable writers before we entered law school. Then the roof fell in.

One problem in law school is that we read older cases by dead judges. Of course, Cardozo, Holmes, and Jackson were great writers, but most judges are not, especially the older ones. I randomly selected an Ohio Supreme Court case from 1946, with this first paragraph:

> The appellant complains that the trial court erred in holding that an attorney at law representing a loan association in the distribution of the proceeds of a loan to be made by such association could refuse to answer questions concerning such distribution on the ground that to answer would disclose a confidential communication to his client; and that the trial court erred in holding that a garnishee ordered by the court to appear for examination as to his indebtedness to the judgment debtor was the witness of the judgment creditor and could not be called for cross-examination by the latter.[2]

This is not the worst example; it is just random. But it could be translated into plain English fairly easily. Restated, it could be two sentences and contain about half

2. *Peoples Bank & Savings Co. v. Katz* (1946), 146 Ohio St. 207, 65 N.E.2d 708.

of its now 100 words. If the writer's goal was to write an exactly 100-word sentence, the goal was reached. If the goal was communication, the sentence was a total failure.

It is not just that many judges write badly. Cases are selected for casebooks not because they are examples of good writing, or even clarity, but because they illustrate the precepts of law in that course. Even when edited, many of these cases are wordy, redundant, and confusing. Perhaps there is value for the law student in this situation—it is training to pick out the needle of law from the haystack of verbiage. But the inadvertent consequence of reading all this lawspeak and generally bad writing is that it causes the student to internalize it. We think that if judges write this way, then it is the language of the profession—something to be emulated.

The problem is compounded exponentially by law students' encounters with other legal writing—leases, contracts, pleadings—some hardly changed from Norman times. Then there is also the red meat of the law—statutes. For sheer unfathomability, statutes are probably the champions.

Here is an Ohio example:

Subject to division (B)(4) of this section, if, within six years of the offense, the offender has been convicted of or pleaded guilty to one violation of division (A) or (B) of section 4511.19 of the Revised Code, a municipal ordinance relating to operating a vehicle while under the influence of alcohol, a drug of abuse, or alcohol and a drug of abuse, a municipal ordinance relating to operating a motor vehicle with a prohibited concentration of alcohol in the blood, breath, or urine, section 2903.04 of the Revised Code in a case in which the offender was subject to the sanctions described in division (D) of that section, section 2903.06 or 2903.08 of the Revised Code, former section 2903.07 of the Revised Code, or a municipal ordinance that is substantially similar to former section 2903.07 of the Revised Code in a case in which the jury or judge found that the offender was under the influence of alcohol, a drug of abuse, or alcohol and a drug of abuse, or a statute of the United States or of any other state or a municipal ordinance of a municipal corporation located in any other state that is substantially similar to division (A) or (B) of section 4511.19 of the Revised Code, the judge shall suspend the offender's driver's or commercial driver's license or permit or nonresident operating privilege for not less than one year nor more than five years.[3]

---

3.   R.C. 4507.16(B)(2).

This is just an average example of drafting clarity. A 239-word sentence is unreadable, which should come as no news. I have examples of 400+ words in a single statutory sentence, but no room (or desire) to include them here.

If the exposure to indecipherable writing in law school were not bad enough, then the young lawyer ventures forth into the "real world" of law practice. Many years ago I taught legal drafting. One of my students took what I said to heart. She was working part-time for a big firm. She wrote a memorandum for a senior partner. It was returned with "make it more lawyerlike"—that is, make it more unreadable by inserting legal jargon, passive voice, nominalization, and other traits of legal writing.

Old ideas die hard. Legal writing has been bad for a long time. For an entertaining and educational explanation, read Peter Tiersma's book, *Legal Language*,[4] which gives a fascinating history of how we got to the present state.

As lawyers, what we do most is write. Lincoln said that lawyers' time and advice are our stock in trade, but we

4. Tiersma, Legal Language (1999).

express the advice in words. And we use much of our time in writing—in communicating by the written word. Sometimes, though, we fail to remember the first object of writing—to communicate.

The theme of this short book is writing in plain language. The plain-language movement has many champions, and is slowly winning over lawyers, professors, practitioners, and even judges. Bryan Garner, the noted lecturer on legal writing, author of many books on the subject, and editor-in-chief of the recent editions of *Black's Law Dictionary*, is my personal hero. You should always keep his book *Dictionary of American Legal Usage* on your desk. Garner's other books, and those of other writing gurus, are listed in the Bibliography. This book offers just a short sample of what is available. You should, after reading this book, graduate to the more comprehensive works.

Writing is a skill that can be learned—not that any of us can learn to be a Cardozo or a Holmes—or Elmore Leonard. But we can substantially improve our communication by learning a few skills, a few tricks, and unlearning some "rules" that get in the way of good writing.

Otherwise, we end up writing like this:

Due to the fact that the plaintiff-appellant had up to this point in time supplied an insufficient number of widgets, defendant-appellee specified that, in the event that an insufficient number was supplied in the future, the contract would be held to be terminated, and deemed to be null and void and of no further effect.

Or this:

Based on the findings and conclusions set forth with respect to each of the four areas of primary concern discussed above, the facts disclosed through our preliminary investigation do not, in our judgment, warrant a further widespread investigation by independent counsel and auditors.

Four months later, Enron collapsed.

Or this:

For the purposes of the traffic code, the words and phrases defined in the sections hereunder shall have the meanings therein respectively ascribed to them unless a different meaning is clearly indicated by the context.[5]

---

5. Cincinnati Municipal Code 501-1.

Translation: It means what it says unless it doesn't.

Or this:

> Procedural Posture: This action arises from the flooding, on June 19, 1998, of a single-family home in which Plaintiffs resided with raw sewage.

Sometimes, we just don't read what we write.

Or this:

> In other words, the Court in reaching its decision (to grant Plaintiff-Appellee's Motion for Summary Judgment and denying Defendant-Appellant's Motion for Summary Judgment) used arguments in Defendant-Appellant's memorandum in its Motion for Summary Judgment and Defendant-Appellant's memorandum in its Motion to Dismiss. (The Motion to Dismiss was granted and Plaintiff-Appellee was required to file an amended complaint.)

This is from a real brief filed in our court. Translation: Who knows?

But we are not alone. For sheer unfathomability, academics can sometimes exceed us:

The move from a structuralist account in which capital is understood to structure social relations in relatively homologous ways to a view of hegemony in which power relations are subject to repetition, convergence, and rearticulation brought the question of temporality into the thinking of structure, and marked a shift from a form of Althusserian theory that takes structural totalities as theoretical objects to one in which the insights into the contingent possibility of structure inaugurate a renewed conception of hegemony as bound up with the contingent sites and strategies of the rearticulation of power.

Scores a perfect zero on any readability test.

Later we will discuss readability statistics. Program your word processor to show these. In Word, they are an option button on spellcheck.

Now let's see if we can go about correcting some of these old habits.

**"Is that just a suggestion,
or really more of a law?"**

Rules of Legal Writing

In this book I propose forty rules to improve legal writing. Forty is an arbitrary number—the first edition had thirty. There could be five hundred. Because this is a primer, I have limited it to a manageable number.

I use "rules" because that seems about midway between "laws" and "suggestions." They are not laws, because some can be broken, and many must be fit to the specific task at hand. But you should know why you are breaking them. They are a bit more than suggestions— many you may disregard only at your peril.

Rule 1
Know Your Audience

In all writing, as in speaking, the first rule is to know your audience. If you are communicating to a court, know the court—be familiar with the local rules and practices, the members of the court, and the preferences of those individuals.

Who are you writing for? Are you writing a brief for an appellate court, a trial brief, an opinion letter to in-house counsel, a letter to a highly knowledgeable layperson, or one to an unsophisticated client? Obviously, you would not write the same way to these different audiences.

If the judge is an expert on the law on your issue, then the facts are all the judge should need to process the argument—the facts become most important. If you are before a brand-new judge who practiced probate law for twenty years, then you will probably assume that the judge's knowledge of the law of your trade-secrets case might be less. Then, your brief should contain a more fundamental discussion of the law.

We are here concerned mainly with persuasive writing—transaction drafting and legislation can present particular problems, but they also should be in plain language. That battle is for another day, however. In this book, we are concerned mainly with persuasive writing.

If you are to persuade a judge to rule in your favor, or an adversary's lawyer to pay you money or to demand less money, you want to be persuasive. And the most important step is communicating clearly what it is you are trying to persuade the other person to do.

Rule 2
Front-Load Your Document— Context Before Detail

As with all writing, organize your document to be front-loaded; that is, educate the reader as to what is coming. Put the important material up front.

Readers understand much more easily if they have a context. Because readers understand new information in relation to what they already know, tell them a piece of new information that relates to their presumed knowledge. Then build on that information with each new piece you add.

First, ask yourself how much your audience already knows about the facts and the law of your case. The answer is that the judge knows very little about the facts of your case. You may have lived with your case for years, but the judge knows only what is set out in the pleadings until you explain what happened.

Strive to explain the case in a way that an average person can understand. Judges and lawyers are generally sophisticated readers and can understand difficult prose if given enough time. But why would you want to make it difficult? Each extra step the reader must take in deciphering the facts of your case or the theory of your argument distracts from the force of your presentation. Make it easy for the reader.

Explain your case in the first two or three pages—including a statement of the issues and then the facts. If you cannot explain the essence of the dispute in three pages, you probably have already lost your first and best chance to keep the reader's attention.

You must build a container—context—in the reader's mind, so when you pour in the facts and the law of your case, the reader has the container to hold the information. Otherwise, it leaks out.

How do you read legal opinions? Too often, you have to skip to the end to find out what happened. An appellate opinion should be written so that the first paragraph or two tells you about the case and its outcome. So should your brief or memorandum. Tell the court what you want to happen.

One reason we put important points up front is that we need to put context before details. The reader learns by building on prior knowledge. If the reader starts with no knowledge of your case—which is generally true—you have to give the reader everything. Do not start out giving facts about your case without giving the context. Tell the reader what kind of case it is. And the most important part of putting context before detail is framing the issue—letting the reader know what the case is about. Put that right up front.

Rule 3
Frame the Issue in Fewer than 75 Words

Before you start in with facts, procedure, or anything else, tell the reader what the case is about. The most important part of your trial or appellate brief, or even of a memorandum to another lawyer or a letter to a client, is framing the issue. What is the question you are trying to answer for the court, the other lawyer, or the client? What do you want the court to decide?

Do not start writing your brief or memo until you have a succinct statement of what the case is about. And you must do this in 50-75 words. If you can't explain the case in 75 words, you do not understand it very well, and neither will your reader. Too often I have seen cases go all the way to appeal without the lawyers having figured out what the case is about.

Put your issue statement right up front, preferably in the first paragraph of your brief or memo. This is the best lesson I learned from attending my first Bryan Garner seminar.

Here are three examples:

Paula Jones was fired from her job with Environmess, Inc. because she consulted a lawyer about a possible slip-and-fall case against an Environmess client. If Ohio workers may only enter the courthouse in fear of losing their livelihood, they cannot exercise any of their legal rights. But Ohio law mandates that the courthouse door must remain open.

(57 Words)

Ohio workers' compensation coverage does not extend to a Canadian citizen residing in Kentucky and injured in Illinois while engaged exclusively in interstate commerce under an employment contract entered into in Florida with a Florida employer.

(36 Words)

Mowing the grassy portion of a parcel of land for over 21 years—while using the other portion for parking—constitutes adverse possession of the entire parcel.

(27 Words)

A short, plain statement of the issue tells the reader what the case is about and provides context for the discussion that follows. It also defines the issue in a manner that, if the court accepts your framing, will allow you to win.

At a seminar someone asked, "How can I do that when the court rules specify a format—and make me put the 'procedureal posture' first? Should I put the 75 words next?"

Some courts do specify what you have to put in—ours does. But our rules don't prohibit you from putting a "Statement of the Case" right up front. Put it before any other text!

Rule 4
State the Facts Succinctly

Remember that you have already put the issue up front in 75 or fewer words. Then in your facts statement, you have to explain the case fully.

One can make a good argument that the statement of facts is the most important part of your memo or brief. I think I know something about the law, so I read the facts first—often, I then know what's coming (or should be) in the legal argument.

Be honest, but state the facts in a manner calculated to have the reader come to the conclusion you want. If the judge reading the brief immediately thinks "Hey, they can't do that," (you hope about your opponent) you are halfway to winning.

You have already told the reader what the issue is and generally what kind of case it is in your 75-word—or 57-word—statement. Then expand on that. A facts statement of two or three pages should suffice. After you have done your short statement of facts, you can weave additional facts into the discussion section of your document—you can add and expand there if you need to. Your first statement is to give context—a roadmap.

Have a non-lawyer (perhaps a teenager) read your facts statement and see if that reader can tell you what the case is about. (Yes, you may, and often should, end a sentence with a preposition.) If a non-lawyer cannot understand the facts of your case, you have failed.

Be concise. Advertising and speech writers know that strong writing comes from paring words to a minimum. The fewer the words, the more memorable the point:

"I have nothing to offer but blood, tears, toil, and sweat."
"I have a dream."
"Where's the beef?"

Rule 5
Avoid Overchronicling—
Most Dates Are Clutter

There is nothing wrong with stating the facts in chronological order. Your initial outline of the case should list all dates—you don't yet know what dates are going to be important. But when you write your brief or memo, do not fall into the habit of starting every sentence with a date.

Avoid overchronicling. Too many briefs start out by reciting a chronology of facts: "On March 23, 2000, this happened, then on May 6, 2000, this happened." This approach confuses the readers, because we don't know what facts are important, and what, if any, dates we should remember. As a general rule, most dates are not important.

Puting in an exact date signals to the reader that *this date is important—remember it—you will need it later.*

Unless an exact date is important—as in a statute-of-limitations issue—leave it out. Instead, tell us only the material facts, and why they are important.

Judges overchronicle too. I saw a case where 12 straight paragraphs started with the date: "On May 23, 2001 . . . . On June 1, 2001 . . . ." I just couldn't bring myself to wade through the case.

You can maintain continuity and order by clues like *next* and *later*, or *next month*.

Say *in June* rather than on *June 14, 2000*. And remember that *June 2004* does not take a comma.

Even worse is the expression *on or about*—if you have been working on the case for years, you should know when events happened.

Rule 6
No Parenthetical Numerals

Especially irritating is the practice of spelling out numbers and then attaching parenthetical numericals—a habit learned when scribes used quill pens to copy documents. The real reason for this was to prevent fraud by making it difficult to alter documents. But in typescript, *four* and *seven* are unlikely to be confused.

Lawyers commonly write "There are four (4) plaintiffs and six (6) defendants, all claiming the ten thousand dollars ($10,000). But only three (3) of the four (4) plaintiffs are entitled to recover from one (1) defendant."

The reader automatically repeats the numbers. It is extremely hard to read and looks silly. Unless you are writing your document in longhand—and unless you believe the judge will alter your numbers—skip this "noxious habit."[6]

In your next Sunday paper, look at the coupons. You'll probably see something like this:

6.   Garner, A Dictionary of Modern Legal Usage (2nd Ed.1995) 606.

Do we think that without the parentheticals the reader would be confused? My guess is that the ad department had to "run it by legal" and that the legal department, being composed of lawyers, inserted the numbers. Ugh.

Most coupons have these superfluous words or numbers, but some companies (Procter & Gamble is one) have clear ones. (Maybe they didn't go through the legal department—or they had lawyers who know about plain English.)

This is my favorite good example:

Do we think consumers will be confused by the lack of the *one* ?

Spell out numbers ten or below (in Ohio). Use numerals for those greater than ten. There are many conflicting rules about when numericals or words are used. Check your own state's format.

Rule 7
Headings Are Signposts— They Should Inform

As part of the "container" you are building in the reader's mind, have headings that tell the reader what is coming. If possible, headings should convey information. "Facts" is better than no heading, but it conveys no information. "The Fire and Aftermath" tells the reader the nature of the facts that are coming.

Headings are signposts that guide the reader. If the legal-argument portion of your document is five pages, you may not need to break it up; but if it is longer, separate it into numbered headings. And why not use the headings to persuade?

Headings do not just give context, they also signal the reader when to safely take a break. The reader needs breaks in digesting complex material. Separate the parts— and subparts—into headings. And remember to use a sans serif font for headings (see Rule 9).

Examples:

I. The Fire and the Aftermath

II. Jones Talks to a Lawyer—And is Fired

III. A Hurdle Too High (The case was about horses.)

The argument section of your brief or memo can have even more substantive headings, stating your position on the legal issue.

I. Mowing the Grassy Portion of a Parcel of Land for over 21 Years and Using the Other Portion for Parking Proves Adverse Possession.

II. The Court's Failure to Warn Singh of the Consequences of His Plea Proved Prejudicial—He Awaits Deportation.

Rule 8
Write Short Paragraphs

Short paragraphs give the reader a chance to pause and digest what has gone before. Just like headings and short sentences, short paragraphs provide a break. If you put three or four sentences with new information in each paragraph, that is enough. Long paragraphs are daunting. Here is an example from a recent Ohio case:

> The basic underlying concept in these cases is that a physician-patient relationship, and thus a duty of care, may arise from whatever circumstances evince the physician's consent to act for the patient's medical benefit. The physician-patient relationship being consensual in nature, these courts recognize that physicians who practice in the institutional environment may be found to have voluntarily assumed a duty of supervisory care pursuant to their contractual and employment arrangements with the hospital. Unlike the traditional personalized delivery of health care, where the patient seeks out and obtains the services of a particular physician, the institutional environment of large teaching hospitals incorporates a myriad of complex and attenuated relationships. Here the presenting patient enters a realm of full-service coordinated care in which technical agreements and affiliations

proliferate the specialized functions and designated obligations of various allied health professionals. In this reality, the responsibility for resident supervision that rests generally with the hospital is often delegated to or assumed by an individual physician or group of physicians. It is their level of skill and competence that ensures adequate patient care. When a patient enters this setting, he or she has every right to expect that the hospital and adjunct physicians will exercise reasonable care in fulfilling their respective assignments. So it is a logical and reasonable application of the principles set forth in *Tracy*, 58 Ohio St.3d 147, 569 N.E.2d 875, to find that a physician may agree in advance to the creation of a physician-patient relationship with the hospital's patients.

(251 Words, 8 sentences 31 words per sentence)

The average reader will balk at tackling such a long paragraph. Breaking it up would allow much better communication.

There is no rule on how many sentences should be in a paragraph. Usually three or four is enough. And you can have a one-sentence paragraph—for emphasis.

Remember each new piece of information should build

on the old.   You have probably seen paragraphs dia-grammed so that each sentence refers back to something in the last sentence.   That is called building on context—building on prior knowledge.

"Form is not something added to substance as a mere protuberant adornment. The two are fused into a unity."

Benjamin Cardozo

Rule 9
Form Is Important—
Make it Look Good

Obviously, the substance of the case is most important—but to communicate the substance, use the best form possible.

It is so much easier nowadays to make the document look good. Remember the old days of typewriters—there were only two type styles, and margins were difficult to change. Now our documents can look great! Use at least one-inch margins. (Our court uses 1.25.) And use an easy-to-read typeface.

Just about the most unreadable font is `Courier`. It was necessary in typewriter days, because each letter had to fit the same size space. But even then, when we wanted—or a court required—something more readable, we used a typesetter and printer. Did you ever see a book printed in `Courier`?

Now, we can do the printing from our desk; but we do not always get it right. For example, I have seen firms spend hundreds of thousands of dollars on technology only to make their briefs and other documents look like they were typed on a 1940 Underwood. Never use Courier.

Use a serif type for text—because the serifs direct the reader's eyes to the next letter. We read horizontally. At least in America, a serif type is best for text.

Times New Roman is the standard now, probably because Microsoft selected it as the default font on Word. But you don't have to follow Microsoft everywhere. One problem with Times New Roman is that the punctuation marks, especially periods and commas, are too small. That is because the type was designed for the *London Times*. In a newspaper the ink bleeds to make a bigger period. But on our printers, the periods and commas don't bleed.

Times is also a very condensed type. Other examples of serif fonts are Georgia, Garamond (I find that Garamond prints too lightly), Book Antiqua, and Palatino. This book is in Palatino. Georgia was designed for the Internet, so is much more readable—it's also bigger. Our court now uses 11.5-point Georgia. Court rules may require 12-point type.

A non-serif, or sans serif, type is good for headings because it directs the reader's eyes downward to the material following the heading. Arial is a common sans serif type. Use it or a similar font for titles or headings. And do not use ALL CAPITALS. Even though all capitals are bigger, they are much more difficult to read than capitals and lower-case letters. That is because we are used to seeing the letters that go above the line, b, l, t, k—and ones that go below—p, q, y, j. Part of our reading is making out the letters by their shape. All caps negates this.

If you want to emphasize, use **bold** or *italics*, but use either very sparingly—you want your words and sentences themselves to provide emphasis, not artificial devices. Technically, italics are harder to read, so bold is better for emphasis.

This is one area where you can occasionally deviate from the rules. Sometimes, different typefaces are acceptable; but if you are going to use a fancy face, know why you are doing it. In formal papers, stick to the basics. If you are doing a brochure or a presentation document, you can experiment more. Those documents typically don't contain large blocks of text, so readability isn't that much of an issue.

Rule 10
Check Your Document Carefully— and Count the Pages

Check every page of every paper that leaves your desk.

Should we really have to make this into a rule? Unfortunately, yes. It is amazing how many times I see briefs with pages upside down or in the wrong order—or missing or blank pages. It certainly breaks up the flow of your argument.

The copy machine may need a new cartridge—but it is the end of the day—or a deadline approaches. The original copy you sign might look great, but the copy the judge gets may be too light to read. I once gave a talk in Cleveland and made this observation. Two young lawyers in the front row started nodding their heads vigorously. Later, they told me they were law clerks from the Third Appellate District, and that too-light pages were a constant problem for them. Make it easy on the reader!

Your clerical staff may be good, but they are capable of mistakes. And the mistakes appear as yours.

Rule 11
Keep It Short—the Page Limit Is Your Friend

Lawyers writing for most courts, especially appellate courts, have a page limit imposed upon them. Most lawyers hate the page limit.

But the page limit is your friend; it requires you to refine your argument. You must strive to write succinctly. It is much harder to write a short brief than a long one. Too much space is a temptation to write all (or more than) you know about the subject.

Make every word count and your document will be much more convincing—the reader might think that you know more than you have written, not less.

At least in our appellate court, we rarely write more than 15 pages to decide a case, and most decisions are shorter. There may be a complex case that takes up to thirty pages, but I don't remember any that are more; and we have to explain both sides' arguments.

The Great Footnote Battle

Now, we come to the most exciting of legal writing topics—footnotes.

Rule 12
Use No Talking Footnotes

If something is important enough to be in a footnote, it is important enough to be in the text. Footnotes detract from readability. Encountering a footnote is like going downstairs to answer the door while making love—it detracts from the endeavor at hand.

Don't let footnotes swallow the page from the bottom, as in a law review article. Law reviews sometimes have about five lines of text with the rest of the page in footnotes. And the footnotes talk to one another—in one article I read, footnote 20 referred to footnote 320. I was happy that I would not run out of footnotes. Your goal is to communicate, not to build a resume. If you make your document look like a law review article, it will be just as unreadable, and as unread.

Many years ago, courts used no footnotes. But then there were very few citations either. Now, we have myriad citations and clutter our prose with them, making legal briefs, memos, and decisions almost impossible to read. Worse, we load all kinds of extraneous material into footnotes.

Whenever I see a brief with expository footnotes, I remember high school, when we were told that we had to have a certain number of footnotes. If we took down something on a note card, we put it in, whether or not it had any relevance to the subject of the paper.

Using "talking" footnotes detracts from readability. Never use them. Never.

The only proper use for footnotes is to give citations, rather than having citations in the middle of a sentence.

Footnotes should be for reference only. If something is truly parenthetical but you believe it needs to be mentioned, use parentheses—that is what they are for.

Rule 13
Citations Go in Footnotes

Lawyers long ago forfeited much readability by including cites in the body of the text, rather than in footnotes. Cluttering up your document with jumbles of letters and numbers makes it almost totally unreadable—for lawyers and laypeople alike. This practice should cease, especially now that footnoting references is simple.

As lawyers, we train ourselves to fast-forward past citations in the body of a document. But it is a very difficult way to read.

Citations belong in footnotes. You will be amazed at the increased readability. The clutter of letters and numbers in the middle of a paragraph is gone. The sentences flow into each other, instead of being isolated islands in a sea of citations.

The change is coming. Four of our six Ohio First District judges are now doing this in opinions. The practice is spreading to other Ohio appellate districts, for which I claim some credit, having given a presentation to most of my colleagues in June 2001.[7] I cannot overemphasize how much better it is to put your citations in footnotes.

One caution, though, is that if you have a seminal case that you will refer back to, you have to put the case name in the body. Then put the citation in a footnote.

But make sure you put only citations in footnotes; that is, use no "talking footnotes." The reader must know that it is unnecessary to read the footnotes—they are for reference only. Constant glancing up and down is not neces-

7. See, *State v. Nguyen*, 157 Ohio App.3d 427, 2004-Ohio-2879, 811 N.E.2d 1180 (6th Dist., Handwork, J.); *State v. Carter*, 157 Ohio App.3d 689, 2004-Ohio-3372, 813 N.E.2d 78 (1st Dist., Hildebrandt, J.); *In re J.S.*, 157 Ohio App.3d 427, 2004-Ohio-2328, 809 N.E.2d 684 (8th Dist., Blackmon, J.); *State v. Pasqua*, 157 Ohio App.3d 427, 2004-Ohio-2992, 811 N.E.2d 601 (1st Dist., Sundermann, J.); *Cleveland v. Atkins*, 156 Ohio App.3d 482, 2004-Ohio-1118, 806 N.E.2d 1007 (8th Dist., Kilbane, J.); *DeCesare v. Bd. of Edn.*, 154 Ohio App.3d 644, 2003-Ohio-5349, 798 N.E.2d 632 (11th Dist., O'Neill, J.); *Turek v. Vaughn*, 154 Ohio App.3d 612, 2003-Ohio-4473, 789 N.E.2d 632 (3d Dist., Walters, J.); *Hollingsworth v. Time Warner Cable*, 157 Ohio App.3d 539, 2004-Ohio-3130, 812 N.E.2d 976 (1st Dist., Winkler, J.); *Westfield v. OKL Can Line*, 155 Ohio App.3d 747, 2003-Ohio-7151, 804 N.E.2d 45 (1st Dist., Painter, J.); *State v. Suber*, 150 Ohio App.3d 200, 2002-Ohio-6309, 779 N.E.2d 1090 (3d Dist., Hadley, J.).

sary. "If footnotes were a rational form of communication, Darwinian selection would have resulted in the eyes being set vertically . . .."[8]

Let's see the difference. This is from a 1998 Ohio Supreme Court case:

> The legislative process and accountability are the cornerstones of the democratic process which [sic—*which* should be *that*] justify the General Assembly's role as lawmaker. In contrast, administrative rules do not dictate public policy, but rather expound upon public policy already established by the General Assembly in the Revised Code. "The purpose of administrative rulemaking is to facilitate an administrative agency's placing into effect a policy declared by the General Assembly in the statutes to be administered by the agency." *Doyle v. Ohio Bur. of Motor Vehicles* (1990), 51 Ohio St.3d 46, 47, 554 N.E.2d 97, 99, quoting *Carroll v. Dept. of Adm. Serv.* (1983), 10 Ohio App.3d 108, 110, 10 OBR 132, 133, 460 N.E.2d 704, 706. Yet determination of public policy remains with the General Assembly. *State ex. rel. Bryant v. Akron Metro. Park Dist. For Summit Cty.* (1929), 120 Ohio St. 464, 479, 166 N.E. 407, 411-412, affirmed *State ex rel. Bryant v. Akron Metro Park Dist. for Summit Cty.* (1930), 281 U.S. 74, 50 S.Ct. 228, 74 L.Ed. 710. Administrative agencies may make only

---

8.   Mikva, Goodbye to Footnotes (1985), 56 U.Col.L.Rev. 647, 648.

"subordinate" rules. *Belden v. Union Cent. Life Ins. Co.* (1944), 143 Ohio St. 329, 342-343, 28 O.O. 295, 301, 55 N.E.2d 629, 635-636; see, also, *Redman v. Dept. of Indus. Relations* (1996), 75 Ohio St.3d 399, 404, 662 N.E.2d 352, 357; *Blue Cross of Northeast Ohio v. Ratchford* (1980), 64 Ohio St.2d 256, 259, 18 O.O.3d 450, 452, 416 N.E.2d 614, 617.

Look at the difference when we remove the clutter of citations:

The legislative process and accountability are the cornerstones of the democratic process which [sic] justify the General Assembly's role as lawmaker. In contrast, administrative rules do not dictate public policy, but rather expound upon public policy already established by the General Assembly in the Revised Code. "The purpose of administrative rulemaking is to facilitate an administrative agency's placing into effect a policy declared by the General Assembly in the statutes to be adminis-tered by the agency."[1] Yet determination of public policy remains with the General Assembly.[2] Administrative agencies may make only "subordi-nate" rules.[3]

1. *Doyle v. Ohio Bur. Of Motor Vehicles* (1990), 51 Ohio St.3d 46, 47, 554 N.E.2d 97, 99, quoting *Carroll v. Dept. of Adm. Serv.* (1983), 10 Ohio App.3d 108, 110, 10 OBR 132, 133, 460 N.E.2d 704, 706.

2. *State ex. rel. Bryant v. Akron Metro. Park Dist. For Summit*

> *Cty.* (1929), 120 Ohio St. 464, 479, 166 N.E. 407, 411-412, affirmed *State ex rel. Bryant v. Akron Metro Park Dist. For Summit Cty.* (1930), 281 U.S. 74, 50 S.Ct. 228, 74 L.Ed. 710.
>
> 3. *Belden v. Union Cent. Life Ins. Co.* (1944), 143 Ohio St. 329, 342-343, 28 O.O. 295, 301, 55 N.E.2d 629, 635-636; see, also, *Redman v. Dept. of Indus. Relations* (1996), 75 Ohio St.3d 399, 404, 662 N.E.2d 352, 357; *Blue Cross of Northeast Ohio v. Ratchford* (1980), 64 Ohio St.2d 256, 259, 18 O.O.3d 450, 452, 416 N.E.2d 614, 617.

The passage now makes sense and can be easily understood. The citations are in footnotes at the bottom of the page, and readers do not need to look at them unless they want to look up the cases. The footnotes can be in smaller type, thus saving a great deal of space in your document.

Bryan Garner did an excellent article on the plague of citations in text—*Clearing the Cobwebs from Judicial Opinions*—in *Court Review*, the magazine of the American Judges Association.[9] More and more judges across the country are taking up the cause.

I rest my case.

---

9. Garner, Clearing the Cobwebs from Judicial Opinions (Summer 2001), Court Review 4.

Rule 14
Use the Proper Form of Citation–Ohio's New System

Whatever court you write for, use the local system of citation. Readers from outside Ohio may skip this section.

If you are writing for an Ohio court, use the Ohio Supreme Court system of citation. For whatever reason, Ohio has its own form, not the Uniform System. (The "Bluebook" is only used when the Ohio form doesn't cover an issue.) The Association of Legal Writing Directors puts out a better system of citation,[10] but Ohio specifies the Bluebook, so we have to use it.

Ohio's system is not wholly different—the most immediately apparent change is that the date comes before the reporter, e.g., *The Cincinnati Enquirer v. Cincinnati* (2001), 145 Ohio App.3d 335, 762 N.E.2d 1057. But that is changing. Note that there is no space between App. and 3d—the period serves as separation. Also, many words are abbreviated in case names.

---

10. The ALWD Citation Manual: A Professional System of Citation (2000).

A New System

The Ohio Supreme Court has changed the citation format and citation rules effective May 2002.

Since May 1, 2002, all Ohio appellate court opinions, all Ohio Supreme Court opinions, and all trial court decisions designated for publication are permanently posted on the supreme court's website. This repository of opinions not only provids a useful tool for litigants, but it also helps streamlines citation practices.

The new rules require each paragraph to be numbered, facilitating the location of pinpoint citations. Unfortunately, the numbering system specifies that the numbers be in 12-point bold type {¶55}, thus adding visual clutter to each paragraph. Surely, the paragraph number could be in the margin, and in smaller and lighter type. It will be just another thing we will have to train our eyes to fast-forward around, like the citations that some judges still put in the text of opinions, rather than in footnotes where they belong.

Citations must now include the website citation, in addition to a print citation, if available. A sample is *State v. Were*, 94 Ohio St.3d 171, 2002-Ohio-481, 761 N.E.2d 591, at ¶15.

There is now no need for the date, because the first part of the web citation provides the date. One boon for lawyers, law students, and clerks is that pinpoint page numbers will never be needed—the paragraph numbers will be the same in all versions. Of course, older cases will be cited as before (except the "unreported" designation will be dropped), but the web cites are available now for appellate cases going back to September 2001, and supreme court cases back to 1992. Eventually, all will be on the supreme court site.

Another change is that you now only spell out numbers from one to ten; numbers like 12 are stated in numerials. The previous rule was so weird that I don't even want to explain it. The new rule is much simpler. And *no* Latin words are italicized.

Controlling-Non-Controlling Distinction Abolished

The Ohio Supreme Court has also abolished the distinction between "controlling" and "persuasive" appellate court opinions. Previously, reported (printed) appellate opinions were controlling in their judicial district, but unreported decisions were only persuasive—that is, the trial courts did not have to follow an unreported case.

Recognizing that the prior distinction had failed to keep pace with technological advances, the court found it no longer necessary to maintain the "published-controlling" and "unpublished-persuasive" dichotomy. The new rules rightly acknowledge that the prevalence of online legal resources has rendered the published-unpublished distinction obsolete. The new rule, S.Ct.R.Rep.Op. 4(B), states, "All courts of appeals opinions issued after the effective date of these rules may be cited as legal authority and weighted as considered appropriate by the courts." What is "considered appropriate" is unclear at best. A comment seems to indicate that all cases are now controlling, but that is certainly not the import of the rule itself.

The new rules also modify the syllabus rule, which, like the published-unpublished rule, had outlived its usefulness. Rather than confining the controlling points of law to the Ohio Supreme Court syllabus, the new rules recognize that the law may be found in the syllabus, the text, and the footnotes (though there should not be any "talking" footnotes, much less ones containing new legal holdings). Why would any court hide a rule of law in a footnote? That's just goofy. The syllabus, however, is not altogether abolished, and it still will control over any disharmony with the text.

What do these new rules mean to the brief writer—and to any lawyer citing cases in any context? First, because all opinions may now be cited as legal authority "and weighted as deemed appropriate by the courts," the advocate has a burden to sift through the mountain of precedent and synthesize it for the court. In some cases, the attorney may be called upon to defend the key precedent and to convince the court that it should be given more weight than authority cited by the other party. The committee proposing these rules fully acknowledged this possibility, recognizing that it may now be incumbent on attorneys to isolate "the 'best' precedent."

Second, the rules specifically impose on the brief writer the duty to conduct a "diligent search" concerning the subsequent history of any cited case that is only available electronically and to report any disposition by higher courts. While attorneys should always verify the cases in their briefs, the rules offer a gentle reminder that the new electronic format does not excuse that duty.

Third, brief writers should take advantage of the new electronic format and the numbered paragraphs to provide more accurate pinpoint citations. Far too often, attorneys cite a case to support their argument without even providing a precise page number or an explanation of the relevance of the case. In seeking to persuade a panel of judges, attorneys should not hesitate to direct attention to the precise paragraph that advances their argument. Though the new form of citation will take some getting used to, the benefits are well worth the trouble. And, of course, the new form is not optional, but mandatory.

Ohio is one of the first states to take this approach to judicial opinions, and it may serve as a model for other jurisdictions. While this new world of legal opinions may give some pause, Ohio's attorneys should not view these changes with trepidation. Many courts are experimenting with or making plans to implement on-line filing systems. On-line access to opinions may facilitate electronic briefing with links to the cases cited in the briefs. These technological advances should be welcomed by the bench and bar alike, because they represent an opportunity for attorneys to enhance their brief writing and for judges to perform their jobs more efficiently.

Also, write R.C., not O.R.C. (We know it is Ohio.) Judges are used to reading the proper form. If you deviate, the reader has to make one more translation. Make it easy for the reader. Every reported case in Ohio is published in the Ohio Supreme Court form—your brief or memo should conform.

If you need a copy of the new system of citation, you can download it from www.sconet.state.oh.us/ROD.

Rule 15
Edit, Edit, Edit

Edit, edit, edit, and edit again. Typos, bad grammar, and misplaced paragraphs (which were not such a problem before word processing) simply take away from your argument.

Keep a copy of Bryan Garner's book *A Dictionary of Modern Legal Usage*[11] at your side to answer grammar, syntax, and punctuation questions. Though it's a reference book, it is so good that you might just read it.

With new technology always comes new pitfalls—following the "spellcheck" or "grammarcheck" blindly leads to some weird words and constructions. If you have a staff member do the word processing, it is even more important to read every word. Spellcheck can substitute wrong words—words spelled correctly, but not what you mean.

---

11. Garner, A Dictionary of Modern Legal Usage (2nd Ed. 1995). See, also, Williams, Style: Ten Lessons in Clarity and Grace (4th Ed. 1994); Gordon, The Deluxe Transitive Vampire (1993); Garner, Elements of Legal Style (2nd Ed. 2002); Garner's Modern American Usage (2003). See Bibliography.

You may mean *constitution*, but spellcheck reads it as *constipation*. We always read about *tortuous* interference with contract. And don't even think of the *penal* system or the *public* interest.

Here is an example:

The Supreme Court of Ohio
JUDICIAL COLLAGE
30 EAST BROAD STREET, COLUMBUS, OHIO 43266-0419

I received this on an envelope in the mail a few years ago. *Collage* is a word, but not the one they wanted.

Those of us who do our own writing—or edit by computer—should always do a final edit—do not let your assistant do the final edit with spellcheck without proofing very carefully again. Then, have someone who is not involved proofread again. Proofing your own doesn't always work—we tend to see what we think we have written.

Another hint is to program your spellcheck to highlight *trail* so you can determine if you actually mean *trial*. This is probably the most common mistake we see—*the trail judge* was in error. Happy trails!

The 1818 Rule

Rule 16
Write Short Sentences—
the 1818 Rule
Part I

Write short, crisp sentences. What is the most under-used punctuation mark in legal writing? The period—it is that key down at the lower right of your keyboard. Even though you are a lawyer, you are allowed to use it. The most overused is easy—the comma.

You should strive to average 18 words per sentence, or fewer—hence the *18*, the first part of the 1818 Rule. If you have 19 or 20 words per sentence, you are still okay, but if you get much over 20, you are sacrificing readability.

Long sentences are difficult to read. The reader some-times forgets what the first part of a long sentence said by the end.

The following is just a random example, from the Ohio Supreme Court:

> As indicated immediately above, the legislative history of R.C. 4113.52 clearly reveals that the General Assembly considered and rejected the notion of providing a wider range of statutory civil remedies for qualifying whistleblowers who are discharged or disciplined in violation of the statute. However, this fact alone does not answer the question whether the remedies set forth in R.C. 4113.52 are intended to be exclusive. Nor is the fact that the legislature enacted R.C. 4113.52 in apparent response to *Phung* a persuasive reason to hold that the statute preempts the formation or recognition of an independent cause of action in tort under *Greeley* and its progeny for wrongful discharge in violation of public policy. Indeed, we find nothing in R.C. 4113.52 or its history that compels the conclusion that it was the express will of the General Assembly that any and all causes of action premised on whistleblowing must be commenced and remedied exclusively under R.C. 4113.52. Rather, on the basis of the information available, it is much more reasonable to conclude that the General Assembly enacted R.C. 4113.52 to remedy the defect in the law caused by this court's decision in *Phung*, but never intended to preclude the future development of the common law of this state in the area of "whistle-blowing."

(Average 43 words per sentence!)

The paragraph is long, and its constituent sentences are also extremely long. The reader must take notes to figure out what the court is saying (or attempting to say). If communication is the goal, this paragraph failed.

Statutes are the worst offenders for long sentences:

R.C. 4511.99(A)(10)

Notwithstanding any section of the Revised Code that authorizes the suspension of the imposition or execution of a sentence, the placement of an offender in any treatment program in lieu of imprisonment, or the use of a community control sanction for an offender convicted of a felony, no court shall suspend the ten, twenty, thirty, or sixty consecutive days of imprisonment required to be imposed on an offender by division (A)(2), (3), (6), or (7) of this section, no court shall place an offender who is sentenced pursuant to division (A)(2), (3), (4), (6), (7), or (8) of this section in any treatment program in lieu of imprisonment until after the offender has served the ten, twenty, thirty, or sixty consecutive days of imprisonment or the mandatory term of local incarceration or mandatory prison term of sixty or one hundred twenty consecutive days required to be imposed pursuant to division (A)(2), (3), (4), (6), (7), or (8) of this section, no court that sentences an offender under division (A)(4) or (8) of this section shall impose any sanction other than a mandatory term of local incarceration or mandatory prison term to apply to the offender until after the offender has served the mandatory term of local incarceration or mandatory prison term of sixty or one hundred twenty consecutive days required to be imposed pursuant to division (A)(4) or (8) of this section, and no court that imposes a sentence of imprisonment and a period of electronically monitored house arrest upon an offender under division (A)(2), (3), (6), or (7) of this section shall suspend any portion of the sentence or place the offender in any treatment program in lieu of imprisonment or electronically monitored house arrest.

(288 Words in one Sentence.)

How do we expect people to comply with the law? The Ohio Revised Code is almost totally unreadable. Most other states aren't quite as bad, but all have indecipherable sentences.

Legal writing needs more periods, fewer commas. Again, sentence length should average no more than 18 words. Word processors have a feature that will calculate words-per-sentence—be sure to use it. Remember, readers need to digest. Every separation—sentence, paragraph, or section heading—allows a pause and signifies to the readers that they can tackle the material in digestible portions.

Read Cardozo (usually), Holmes, and Jackson—notice the short, crisp sentences.

Cardozo:

> No answer is it to say that the chance would have been of little value even if seasonably offered. Such a calculus of probabilities is beyond the science of the chancery. Salmon, the real estate operator, might have been preferred to Meinhard, the woolen merchant. On the other hand, Meinhard might have offered better terms, or reinforced his offer by alliance with the wealth of others. Perhaps he might even have persuaded the lessor to renew the Bristol lease alone, postponing for a time, in return for higher rentals, the improvement of adjoining lots.[12]

(18.8 words per sentence.)

Jackson:

> More than 32,000 stockholders are owners of this enterprise. They are domiciled in every state of the

12. *Meinhard v. Salmon* (1928), 249 N.Y. 458, 465, 164 N.E. 545, 547 (Cardozo, J.).

Union, less than 2 per cent of them in Wisconsin. Under the corporation's charter and the applicable law of New Jersey the stockholders may be paid dividends only from its surplus or net profits. Every corporate act connected with payment of dividends takes place in Chicago. There the directors meet to declare them, there the checks are drawn and mailed. They are paid out of the corporation's general funds on deposit in Chicago or New York.[13]

(15.5 words per sentence.)

Holmes:

Coming then to the merits, we are of the opinion that the judgment was right. The interpretation of constitutional principles must not be too literal. We must remember that the machinery of government would not work if it were not allowed a little play in its joints.[14]

(15 words per sentence.)

---

13. *International Harvester Co. v. Wisconsin Dept. of Taxation* (1944), 322 U.S. 435, 446 (Jackson, J., dissenting).
14. *Bain Peanut Co. v. Pinson* (1931), 282 U.S. 499, 501.

Cardozo:

> Plainly on proof of these facts the presumption van-
> ishes that the driver was discharging his duty to the
> master. The character of the transaction is so
> extraordinary, the occupation of the truck by the
> revellers so dominant and exclusive, as to rebut the
> inference that the driver was serving his employer
> at the same time that he was promoting the pleas-
> ure of his friends. The dual function, if it existed,
> can no longer rest upon presumption. Regularity
> will no longer be taken for granted when irregular-
> ity is written over the whole surface of the picture.
> We will no longer presume anything. What the
> plaintiff wishes us to find for him, that he must
> prove.[15]

(19 words per sentence.)

Painter:

> The "attorney's fees" provision was in type this small,
> on the back of a form. The entire page was covered
> by dense type, running from the top of the page to
> the bottom. It was as if the drafter attempted to see
> just how many words could fit on an 8.5" x 11"
> piece of paper. The answer is 4,385, give or take a

15 *Ficco v. Carter* (1932), 234 N.Y. 219, 137 N.E. 309.

few. In contrast, there are 277 words on this page, which is the same size.

The sentence containing the attorney-fee language is ninety-six words long, following a 206-word sentence. Sentences of more than twenty words, especially badly constructed sentences, are very difficult to read. The paragraph contains more than 600 words—this paragraph contains forty-two words.

I agree that this provision, hidden in a haystack of legal jargon and gibberish, is unenforceable. No one could be expected to read or understand—much less bargain over—this contractual provision. If boilerplate language is unreadable and indecipherable, it should be unenforceable, especially by the drafter. A long-standing common-law rule may not be thus abrogated.[16]

(15 words per sentence.)

Long sentences are especially difficult when strung together. Sophisticated readers can understand longer sentences—if they are properly constructed—but no one can wade through ten in a row. Break up the pace—follow a longer sentence with a short one.

16. *Vermeer of S. Ohio, Inc. v. Argo Constr. Co.* (2001), 144 Ohio App.3d 271, 760 N.E.2d 1 (Painter, J., concurring)

Readability is the goal. Keep in mind Will Rogers's all-too-often-true comment about legal writing:

> The minute you read something and you can't understand it, you can almost be sure that it was drawn up by a lawyer. Then if you give it to another lawyer to read and he don't know just what it means, why then you can be sure it was drawn up by a lawyer. If it's in a few words and is plain and understandable only one way, it was written by a non-lawyer.[17]

---

17. Rogers, "The Lawyers Talking," 28 July 1935, in Will Rogers' Weekly Archives 6:243-244 (Steven K. Graggert Ed. 1982), quoted in Shapiro, The Oxford Dictionary of Legal Quotations (1993).

Rule 17
Use Mainly Active Voice—
the 1818 Rule
Part II

Make sure your document has no more than 18% passive-voice sentences.

Passive voice is not forbidden. Sometimes you do not need to name the actor—*Many books have been written on legal writing*. Or a smooth transition from one sentence to the next requires you to put the subject first. Or you might want to hide the actor—*Mistakes were made*.

If you represent the truck driver who ran over the nun in the crosswalk, you will tell the court or the jury, *An accident occurred*. But usually active is better; action is easier to understand. We do not usually talk in passive voice.

In the schoolyard, we could say, *Johnny tried to hit me*. Now, after law school, we would probably say, *An attempt was made by Johnny to perform an assault upon me*. Somehow, the attempt becomes the focus. And we have taken out all the action. This is called nominalization of verbs—taking

a perfectly good action verb and turning it into a noun—
burying the verb in the sentence.

Probably because we, as lawyers, categorize and name
things, *assault* becomes a noun. *A tort was committed.*

Before we became lawyers, we might have expressed
our opinion by saying *I think that.* Now we say, *I am of the
opinion that.* What does it mean to be *of* an opinion? We
have turned a verb, *think,* into a noun, *opinion.*

Or instead of *Smith hit Jones,* we write *Jones was victim-
ized in an assault by Smith.* The verb *hit* becomes the noun
assault. This nominalization creates buried verbs. And it
usually results in a passive-voice sentence—a form of to be
(*was* in the Smith-Jones sentence) becomes the verb.

But it sometimes just adds a verb and obscures the real
verb. Instead of a straightforward *The police searched Smith*
we might say, *The police performed a search upon Smith.* Is
the performance what we want to stress? Of course not;
it's the search. Searched is a fine verb—it conveys exactly
what happened. When we muck it up with a performance,
it is at least distracting—at most misleading.

And when we write *Smith filed a motion for summary*

judgment, we really don't mean to emphasize the filing. If we write *Smith moved for summary judgment,* it makes much more sense and is shorter. Of course, once in a great while, the filing itself is the emphasis, as in *Smith filed his motion five days late.* But not often.

Most nominalizations end with *-tion, -ment, -ence, -ance, -ure, -ery.*

Verb	Noun
determine	determination
advance	advancement
modify	modification
improve	improvement
depend	dependence
divest	divestiture
agree	agreement
admit	admittance
depend	dependence

Nominalizations not only add a noun-verb, they also add an article. So you have two extra words, in addition to taking the action out of the sentence.

Verb	Noun
moved	filed a motion
assumed	made an assumption
prefer	have a preference
reduces	will result in a reduction
violates	is in violation
reduce	make a reduction

Dr. Terri Mester, an English professor at Case Western, uses examples of nominalization in her plain-writing seminars (which are worthwhile, as are mine). My favorite sentence follows, with the nominalizations and passives italicized. "Although *there are* no new natural gas areas that *will be* created, an *enhancement* of land use through *reduction* in flooding *is obtained* through the plan." How about this: "The plan creates no new natural gas areas, but reducing flooding enhances land use." The active-voice revision strikes out 12 useless words (46% of the sentence).

Another of Dr. Mester's examples (all used by permission): "If there is a continuation of this breach, my client will effect an immediate termination of the contract." Revised: "If this breach continues, my client will terminate the contract." This version eliminates eight superfluous words (44%) and strengthens the sentence.

And passive voice can lose a case! One lawyer found out the hard way why passive voice prevents communication. Fraud must be pleaded with particularity. This is what the court said: "Plaintiffs allege that they 'were falsely told that professional golfers such as Fred Couples, Craig Stadler and Fuzzy Zoeller were substantial investors in Ganter USA.' Without any indication of who made this statement to them, however, we can hardly conclude that Plaintiffs have not pleaded this allegation with particularity."[18]

Hunt down passive voice and nominalization. If there is no good reason for using it, put your sentence back the way real people would talk. A number of examples are in the table in Rule 21.

18. *Coroles v. Sabey*, 2003 UT App. 339; 79 P.3d 974.

Rule 18
Use *But* and *And* to Begin Sentences

Do not be afraid to start sentences with *and* or *but*. This signifies good writing. The reason your grammar-school teacher told you not to start a sentence with *and* was because you wrote, *I have a mother. And a father. And a dog.* Use *but* rather than *however* to start a sentence, and see how much better it reads.

Almost any example of good writing pulled at random will contain numerous examples of this rule. *The Wall Street Journal* and *The New York Times* are well-written—look at the front page of either and circle the number of sentences beginning with *and* or *but*. There will be three to ten.

And look at Holmes, for example:

> Courts proceed step by step. And we now have to consider whether the cautious statement in the former case marked the limit of the law . . . . [19]

> But to many people the superfluous is necessary, and it seems to me that Government does not go beyond its

19. *Johnson v. United States* (1913), 228 U.S. 457, 458 (Holmes, J.).

sphere in attempting to make life livable for them.[20]

Or Jackson:

> But we think the previous cases indicate clearly that respondents are within the Act.[21]

Just randomly look at writings you consider good, and you will find countless examples.

Shakespeare:

> Thou hadst, and more, Miranda. But how is it
> That this lives in thy mind? What seest thou else
> In the dark backward and abysm of time?[22]

Pound:

> Hence it is an unjustifiable interference with a natural right. And this is exactly what the court said in an actual case.[23]

---

20. *Tyson & Brother v. Banton* (1927), 273 U.S. 418, 447 (Holmes, J., dissenting).
21. *Armour & Co. v. Wantock* (1944), 323 U.S. 126, 131 (Jackson, J.).
22. Shakespeare, The Tempest, 1.2, 57-59.

Shakespeare again:

> But I am very sorry, good Horatio
> That to Laertes I forgot myself;
> For, by the image of my cause, I see
> The portraiture of his: I'll court his favours.
> But, sure, the bravery of his grief did put me
> Into a towering passion.[24]

If you need even more to convince a backward colleague, just look in any book or article that colleague admits is good writing. You will find *ands* and *buts* at the beginning of many sentences.

23. Pound, The Spirit of the Law and other Writings, (Legal Classics Library ed.1985) 199.
24. Shakespeare, Hamlet, 5.2, 80-85.

Rule 19
Distinguish Between *That* and *Which*

Use *that* restrictively and *which* nonrestrictively. (In Commonwealth English, *which* is used both ways.) That is, if the clause can stand alone, it is preceded by which. If it cannot stand by itself, *that* is appropriate.

Consider the following examples:

The law *that* we follow is just.

The law, *which* is of ancient origin, is the one that we follow.

The court's role is limited to determining the constitutionality of the specific laws *that* the legislature enacts.

But this court can only deal with what we have before us, *which* is an unconstitutional law.

The failure to distinguish appropriately is a common error and one that (not which) I have been guilty of on occasion. But I now have it down, I think. Take my word that the distinction is important.

The easy way to remember is that *which* is preceded by a comma; *that* is not.

Some editors have a penchant for removing unnecessary *thats*. But it is usually better to keep them in, unless you can remove them without opening up any possibility of confusion.

Rule 20
Use the Dash, Parenthesis, and Comma for Degrees of Emphasis

Though you should avoid cluttering up your document with too many incidental comments, sometimes they fit nicely. A dash provides the greatest emphasis—it is the strongest break. Next in degree is the parenthesis, then the comma. If anything, I have overused dashes in this work. But I find them useful. They make a sentence more readable.

Make sure that you use the correct mark for a dash. A dash on an ancient typewriter was two hyphens (- -). In printing, you never saw two hyphens masquerading as a dash. An *em-dash* (word—word) is the proper punctuation now. Your word processor will convert two hyphens to an *em-dash* if you tell it to. Be sure to program it correctly. While you are doing that, also make sure to set it for "smart quotes," which are different at the beginning and end of the quotation.

There is also an *en-dash*, which is slightly longer than a hyphen; it is used in constructions like 1880–1890 (contrast

1880-1890 with a hyphen), or the Lincoln–Douglas debates. But you really will be ahead of the game if you use the *em-dash* properly—if you cheat and use a hyphen for an *en-dash,* no one will notice. But a perfectionist would distinguish.

Rule 21
One Word Is Usually Enough

Do not use two or three or four words for one—*devise and bequeath; grant, bargain, sell, and convey; right, title, and interest; make, ordain, constitute, and appoint*. This goofiness originated with the Norman Conquest in 1066. After that, it was necessary to use both the English and the French words so that all parties could understand. And, of course, "educated" people wrote in Latin, so they sometimes threw that into the mix too.

Have you ever had a client come in for a will (last will and testament) and say, "I'd like to give the rest of my estate to my spouse, the residue to my daughter, and the remainder to my son."? Is there a difference?

If there is no difference between words, don't use more than one. If something is *null*, we assume it is also *void*. If a debt is *due*, it is also *payable*.

We have been doing this since 1066—long since any reason for it existed. Peter Tiersma's book, *Legal Language,* is a fascinating account of the growth of the language of the law, including "Law French" and "Law Latin." Knowing how we came to the sorry state of using too many words is interesting—but doing away with this nonsense is imperative.

Because French nouns usually precede adjectives, we have, for example, malice aforethought, accounts payable, attorney general, condition precedent, and the like. French also gave us the *-ee* and *-or*, as in lessee-lessor, vendee-vendor.[25]

Here are some examples of the confluence of Norman French, Old English, and Latin:

Old English	Old Latin	Old French
Rest	Residue	Remainder
Free		Clear
Will	Testament	
Final	Conclusive	
Fit		Proper
Give, Bequeath		Devise
Sell	Convey	Bargain Grant
Right	Interest	Title

25. See Tiersma, Legal Language 31.

Most of us now understand plain English, but very few of us understand Norman French. Today's French people would not understand Norman French—the language has evolved some in a thousand years. Latin has been dead for centuries, but to the chagrin of students everywhere, it refuses to be buried.

When deciding which of three words to use, always prefer the Anglo-Saxon—the English word. *Sell* is better than *bargain* or *convey*. *Rest* is better than *residue* or *remainder*. Do I strenuously object to the alliteration in *rest*, *residue*, and *remainder*? Not really, but generally avoid more than one word. See *Kohlbrand v. Ranieri* for a discussion of *free and clear*.[26]

A related tendency of lawyers is to use many words when one is more understandable—*sufficient number of = enough; that point in time = then; for the reason that = because*. A longer list follows.

Do not write *filed a motion* unless the filing itself has some significance. *Filed a motion* conjures up in readers' minds someone walking up to the clerk's counter and having a pile of papers stamped. Write *moved*. *Smith moved for summary judgment.*

26. Ohio App.3d 140, 2005-Ohio-295, 823 N.E.2d 76

Do not write *On October 13, 1995, plaintiff-appellant filed a timely appeal to this honorable court*. Again, unless the timeliness or date (or the honor of the court) is in question, you have used so many words for nothing. *Smith appeals* is sufficient, and even that is obvious, and hence unnecessary. Don't write *filed of record*, write *filed*. Where else would it be filed?

Lawyers use too many words in a number of ways: (1) nominalization—*performed a search*; (2) just too many words—*for the reason that*; and (3) passive voice—*it is contended by plaintiff*. Hunt them down. Here are a few examples, and how to fix them.

BAD	BETTER
the means by which	how
entered a contract to	contracted
filed a counterclaim	counterclaimed
filed a motion	moved
filed an application	applied
adequate number of	enough

BAD	BETTER
for the reason that	because
in the event of	if
in light of the fact that	because
notwithstanding the fact that	although
notwithstanding	despite
cause of action	claim
in order to	to
at this point in time	now
until such time as	until
whether or not	whether (usually)
during the month of May	in May
by means of	by
at a later date	later
a distance of five miles	five miles

BAD	BETTER
made a complaint	complained
makes mention of	mentions
utilize	use
period of a week	a week
effectuate	cause
provide assistance	help
is violative of	violates
provide protection to	protect
is of the opinion that	believesis
as a consequence of	because of
made application	applied
made provision	provided
it is contended by plaintiff	plaintiff contends
with regard to	about
in connection with	with

BAD	BETTER
performed a search on	searched
each and every	either "each" or "every"
provide responses	respond
offered testimony	testified
bears a significant resemblance	resembles
reveal the identity of	identify
reach a resolution	resolve
was in conformity with	conformed
effectuate settlement	settle
make inquiry	ask
are in compliance	comply
make allegations	allege
make an examination of	examine

Rule 22
Hyphenate Phrasal Adjectives

The reader is confused by nouns acting as adjectives, or by two adjectives together modifying one noun. Often, the reader will have to back up and read again.

Sentences like these fool the reader:

The public policy exception is rooted. . .
The law abiding citizen. . .

The reader may be fooled into thinking that the public or the law is the subject of the sentence, rather than a modifier of the actual subject. Just add a hyphen, and the reader knows that the hyphenated words are modifiers.

Words that end in -ly are not hyphenated, because they are adverbs—or because the -ly tells the reader that the word is a modifier, not a noun.

Always hyphenate phrases like *wrongful-discharge suit*, or *public-policy exception*. Just take my word for it—the hyphens increase readability.

Rule 23
Always Question "Of"

Write *Ohio Supreme Court,* not *Supreme Court of Ohio.* And there is nothing wrong with the possessive. Write *the court's docke*t, not *the docket of the court.* Somewhere, someone told lawyers not to use possessives, maybe because *docket of the court* sounds more formal than *the court's docket.* It is not. It is just clutter. And much harder to read.

Use the "find" feature on your word processor to hunt down these awkward constructions. Some uses of *of* are fine, but usually, if the word is possessive, just make it so with an apostrophe.

A possessive is fine, as long as the idea is possessive. But a possessive is different than a plural. Lately, everyone but lawyers (but see last paragraph) seems to have fallen into the "creeping apostrophe." This phenomenon does not do away with an *of*; it just adds an apostrophe for no reason, making all plurals into possessives.

Hot Dog's for Sale
Smith & Co., Surveyor's

Hamburger's $1.99
Happy Hour on Friday's
Tuxedo's on Sale

Alas, I can no longer exempt lawyers. One group of lawyers put up a sign on their historic building: *Samuel Hannaford & Sons, Architect's, 1890.*

Rule 24
Always Use the Serial Comma

In a list of three or more, always insert the serial comma. Some writers insist on omitting the last comma, before the "and" or "or." Even *The New York Times* does it. But they are not drafting legal documents. Never omit the last comma—doing so can cause misinterpretation.

Chickens, ducks, and geese is clear. *Chickens, ducks and geese*, allows someone—a lawyer or judge—to assert that *ducks and geese* are a distinct category. Or consider *Smith ordered bacon, eggs and cheese.* Did Smith want eggs mixed with cheese? If you write *Smith ordered bacon, eggs, and cheese* the meaning is clear.

Many cases discuss the problems created by leaving out the serial comma. In some, the court had to search code sections near the legislation in question to determine what, if any, rule the drafter followed.[27] In others, the lack of a serial comma created confusion.[28] In another, the "rule

27. See, e.g., *State ex. rel, Sunshine Enterprises v. Board of Adjustment* (Mo. 2002), 64 S.W. 3d 310.
28. See, e.g., *New York State Dairy Foods, Inc. v. Northeast Dairy Compact Commission* (1999), 198 F.3d 1.

of the serial comma" was debated page after page by majority and dissenting opinions.[29]

Using the serial comma never creates ambiguity, leaving it out sometimes does. So why would you use a construction that is by its nature ambiguous? This is a rule that you may not break.

---

29. *Peterson v. Midwest Security Ins. Co.* (2001), 248 Wis.2d 567, 636 N.E.2d 727.

Rule 25
Avoid Unnecessary Preambles

Cut useless preambles. Unnecessary preambles can weaken or hide the point they introduce. And they add nothing except distraction.

Here are some unnecessary preambles:

Let it be emphasized . . .
It is important to add that . . .
It may be recalled that . . .
It is of significance that . . .
It is interesting to note that . . .
In this regard . . .
Let me say this about that . . .

These phrases add nothing but clutter. In speaking, this type of transition is sometimes necessary to give the listener a break. But it never is in writing.

Rule 26
Purge Lawspeak

Eschew legalese. *Hereinafter, aforesaid,* and the like do not add anything but wordiness and detract from readability. Many studies show that legalese is the number-one complaint of appellate judges and law clerks. *Hereinbeforementioned* is as unreadable as it is silly. Let's stop writing like we were using quill pens, slumped over a Dickensian desk.

This is a rule you cannot break, or even bend. Never, ever, use legalese.

The ancient *now comes plaintiff* [where?], *by and through* [is there a difference?] *his undersigned attorney* is junk. No one reads it anyway. The more clutter and cobwebs you can get out of your document, the more room you have to make your argument.

Cut out *such,* as in *such motion. The* or *that* almost always works. *Pursuant to* usually may be translated as *under.* That is, write *under R.C. 2923.12,* not *pursuant to R.C. 2923.12.* Sometimes, when I'm bored with a brief, I count the number of times *pursuant to* appears.

We have a deal. But both sides put in so many howevers, notwithstandings, and provided thats that I don't know if we really agreed to anything."

Among the many words lawyers overuse looms *provided*. Often it's *provided that*, sometimes *provided also*, sometimes *provided always*. Almost always it's unclear.

As with many legal manglisms, *provided* started out harmlessly enough. It was an enacting word of (very) early legislation. English laws passed by parliament began, *It is provided*. That's OK.

But then lawyers started using *provided* in a different sense—as a *proviso*—meaning an exception. Or a limitation. Or a condition precedent. Or a condition subsequent. Or something. The term became a catch-all lawyerism—"a legal incantation . . . an all-purpose conjunction, invented by lawyers but not known to or understood by grammarians."[30]

Myriad cases turn on what *provided* means. Bryan Garner says it best: "Writers on drafting have long cautioned drafters not to use provisos. In fact, the words *provided that* are a reliable signal that the draft is not going well."

30. Driedger, The Composition of Legislation (2nd ed. 1996) 96, Quoted in Butt & Castle, Modern Legal Drafting (2001) 125.

Don't use *provided that*. Instead, use *if* or *except*, or *when*, or *but*, put one of them first, and rephrase. Or better yet avoid the construction altogether. If you are using provided that to introduce new material, begin a new sentence.

Bad:

The expense may be deducted, provided that it was a business expense.

Better:

If the expense was a business expense, it may be deducted.

Better yet:

If the expense was a business expense, you may deduct it.

Better yet:

You may deduct business expenses.

Bad:

Any person may apply to be a Cincinnati police officer, provided that the person has attained the age of 21.

Better:

Anyone who has attained the age of 21 may apply to be a Cincinnati police officer.

Better yet:

If you are 21 or older, you may apply to be a Cincinnati police officer.

The rewrites aren't perfect—they can probably be improved upon—but they are much better than the originals that use *provided that*. And all the rewrites get much higher readability scores.

Never use *and/or*. This quote should suffice to explain why: "We are confronted with the task of first construing 'and/or,' that befuddling, nameless thing, that Janus-faced verbal monstrosity, neither word nor phrase, the child of a brain of someone too lazy or too dull to express his precise meaning, or too dull to know what he did mean, now commonly used by lawyers in drafting legal documents, through carelessness or ignorance . . ."[31]

31. *Employers' Mut. Liab. Ins. Co. v. Tollefsen* (Wisc.1935), 263 N.W. 376, 377

Rule 27
The Parties have Names

Have you ever represented a client without a name? Only if you represented Prince during a certain period. The parties have names.

Do not go through your whole brief calling parties plaintiff-appellant and defendant-appellee, or the like. Appellant would be enough, but it is much better to call the parties by name. When we use procedural titles, the reader must translate to understand what we mean. When a brief refers to *Plaintiff/Appellant*, I have to think, "Well, that's the side that brought the suit, lost in the trial court, and now wants us to reverse." The procedural titles change throughout the case, but the names remain the same. The names do not require the reader to translate. Just Smith or Jones is fine.

Using names also humanizes your client—even a corporate name; *Smithco*, sounds much more human than *Plaintiff/Appellant/Cross-Appellee*. One brief concerned a dispute between two corporations. The brief called them "the bank" and "the card shop" (the writer's client). It worked well.

Be sure to be consistent and not to switch back and forth between *appellant, Jones,* and *plaintiff.* I recently read a brief that said, "Defendant-Appellant Mary Jones (hereinafter usually referred to as Jones)." Usually? Did that mean she was sometimes Barbara Smith? Gasp.

And just write—once at the beginning—*Plaintiff-Appellant Amalgamated Widgets of North America, Inc. ("Amalgamated"),* not *"hereinafter called"*—no lawspeak. And if your party is John Smith, you may safely call him Smith without first using "John Smith ("Smith")." A great example of unnecessary labeling is the following, taken from a brief in our court:

> The present action stems from injuries suffered by plaintiff/appellant Ann Rogers Smith ("Smith"), on April 22, 2000, after being thrown by her horse in Clippinger Field (the "Field") located in the City of the Village of Indian Hill, Ohio ("Indian Hill"). On that day, Paula Jones ("Jones"), allowed her two Irish Setters ("the dogs")...

There were no other Smiths, Jones, cities, dogs, or fields involved in the case. Each set of parentheses just added more clutter.

Remember, the parties have names, not procedural titles.

Rule 28
Use Quotations Sparingly

I have seen too many briefs composed of strings of quotations and very little else. You should explain how the quoted cases support your theory of the case. Do not use lengthy quotations—a few lines at most. How often do I see something like this:

> The Ohio Court of Appeals for the First District has already held: "To support the defense of discriminatory selective prosecution, the Ohio Supreme Court, independently interpreting Section 2, Article I of the Ohio Constitution pursuant to *Michigan v. Long* (1983), 463 U.S. 1032, 103 S.Ct. 3469, has stated its own two-part test. First, the defendant must show that 'while others similarly situated have not generally been proceeded against because of conduct of the type forming the basis of the charge against him, he is singled out for prosecution.' *State v. Flynt* (1980), 63 Ohio St.2d 132, 134, 407 N.E.2d 15, 17, quoting *United States v. Berrios* (C.A.2, 1974), 501 F.2d 1207, 1211. Second, the defendant must show that the 'selection is "deliberately based upon an unjustifiable standard such as race, religion, or *other arbitrary classification.*"' *Cleveland v. Trzebuckowski* (1999), 85 Ohio St.3d 524, 532, 709 N.E.2d 1148, 1155-1156, citing *State v.*

Wolery (1976), 46 Ohio St.2d 316, 325-326, 348 N.E.2d 351, 358, and quoting Oyler v. Boles (1962), 368 U.S. 448, 456, 82 S.Ct. 501, 506 (emphasis supplied). See, also, *Trzebuckowski* at 534, 709 N.E.2d at 1155, fn. 4. In this case, the city has conceded that it has singled out a particular class for enforcement of the licensing ordinance: those massage establishments and providers that advertise in the 'adult' section of *CityBeat* and adults-only publications. Such advertisements are generally salacious in nature, worded to emphasize the sensual rather than the medicinal rewards of a massage."

See, no one reads long block quotes. People skip that single-space block and go on. Unless the case you are quoting from is exactly on point (very seldom true), just quote the most relevant and persuasive part. And do it in the text if you can.

The Ohio Supreme Court puts all quotes in the body of the text. That helps cut down on long quotes. One reason for this is that the West reporters use a two-column format. Putting in a block indented quote makes the quote only a few words per line. (Unfortunately, that court relented on the rule as applied to appellate opinions. Too bad.)

The column-format problem usually doesn't affect lawyers; but a better reason is that long quotes are not read. Just remember, long blocks are not read. (Yes, I have used some in this book, but usually as bad examples.)

Lead into the quote with your paraphrase of what the quote says. Write, for example, "The Ohio Supreme Court has held that a defendant has no due-process rights." Then put in the quote—no more than three or four lines. The reader might actually read it to see if you are telling the truth. And you have stated your most important point twice.

Be sure to use quotation marks correctly. Misplacing quotation marks is one of the most common mistakes in legal (and other) writing.

In America, all punctuation goes inside the quotation marks, except question marks, semicolons, and exclamation points. A period or comma always goes inside the quotation marks. Always. See Rule 34 for further discussion of quotation marks, with examples.

Rule 29
Use Persuasive Language

Use persuasive language. If you can't explain your case, how can you expect readers to understand it? Examples are always helpful to the reader. Similes or metaphors are very effective to illustrate your analysis.

In a case in our court, the issue was whether a pizza delivery driver was an employee or an independent contractor. One side argued that because the driver used his own car, paid for his own gas, and could use whatever route he wished, he was an independent contractor. The other side stated that servers in the restaurant, admittedly employees, also were not told which way to go between tables to deliver their orders and used their own shoe-leather. Thus, the driver was simply a "waiter on wheels." That phrase found its way into the opinion.[32]

Use examples to illustrate a point:

The exercise of no other fundamental right subjects a citizen to arrest. Should a citizen first go to jail for

32. See *James v. Murphy* (1995), 106 Ohio App.3d 627, 666 N.E.2d 1147.

voting, and be required to prove innocence of multiple voting? Should a citizen first go to jail for marrying, and then get out by proving innocence of bigamy? Should we jail people for publishing a newspaper, then require them to prove that what was published was not libelous or obscene?[33]

Examples make your legal points concrete. Use as many as you think you need. If you can't immediately come up with any absurd results of the court's ruling against your client, keep thinking.

---

33. *Klein v. Leis,* 146 Ohio App.3rd 526, 2002-Ohio-1634, 767 N.E.2d 286.

"No, the firm doesn't have a gym on the premines. But we have so much work for you that you will never miss it."

Rule 30
Continue your Research

Continue your research. You might write a memorandum or a brief months before it is argued before the court.

When some of us started practicing, unreported cases were almost impossible to hunt down. Not anymore. Now you can find almost any case that appeared yesterday.

Check every citation periodically, and again the day before the case is argued, or better yet, the morning of argument. Legal research services have that feature.

It has happened more than once in my tenure that a new Ohio Supreme Court case has appeared in the interim. Or, just as devastating, the court you are arguing before may have decided a case right on point last week. The reply, "I haven't seen that case, your honor," is one you never want to utter.

Rule 31
Hunt Down Adjectives and Adverbs

All of us use adjectives and adverbs too much. Most are unnecessary and detract from the points we are trying to make. Your important noun can sag under the weight of too many adjectives.

Lawyers are fond of *clear* and *clearly*, as *The law is clear that (our side wins)*. Or *Clearly, appellant's argument is meritless*. When a lawyer uses *clear* or *clearly* in a brief, it is most often to introduce the most contested issue in the case. I then think—if the law is so clear, what is the case doing in my court?

Even worse is adding an intensifier—*exceedingly clear*. Part of the problem with this form is that it uses too many words. But the greater issue is weakening the argument. Just as unnecessary preambles (see Rule 25) can weaken your sentence, so can unnecessary adjectives.

Some examples:

BAD	BETTER
extremely important	important, or critical
blatantly untrue	false, or a lie
cold, hard facts	facts
painfully obvious	obvious (or leave out—if something is obvious, you shouldn't need to say so—let the reader come to the conclusion)
exceedingly brilliant	brilliant

Take Anton Chekhov's advice:

Cross out as many adjectives and adverbs as you can. It is comprehensible when I write: "The man sat on the grass," because it is clear and does not detain one's attention. On the other hand, it is difficult to figure out and hard on the brain if I write: "The tall, narrow-chested man of medium height and with a red beard sat down on the green grass that had already been trampled down by the pedestrians, sat down silently, looking around timidly and fearfully." The brain can't grasp all that at once, and art must be grasped at once, instantaneously.[34]

Of course, the painfully obvious redundancies should be scrupulously avoided [read: avoid redundancies]. Something cannot be *very unique* or *absolute best*.

34. Chekhov to Maxim Gorky, 9-3-1899,
http://mockingbird.creighton.edu/NCW/chekwrit.htm

Rule 32
Latin is a Dead Language— Keep it Buried

Use Latin phrases sparingly, if at all. A few—*res ipsa loquitur, respondeat superior*—are acceptable because they are shorthand for much longer concepts. But do not litter your brief or memo with what Daniel Webster called "mangled pieces of murdered Latin."

I saw a case in which the appellate judge, describing what happened in the trial court, wrote that the trial judge had an *ore tenus* hearing. I had to resort to Black's Dictionary; it means *oral* (as opposed to a written or cyber-space hearing?). The judge was trying to impress the reader with his erudition. Instead, he made the reader get up and look up an obscure Latin word, ensuring that the reader lost any train of thought. And engendering a bit of resentment to boot. Remember to make the *reader* feel smart.

When in any doubt, use English. No one will have to go look it up, assuming you use normal English words, which you should always do.

If you must use a Latin word or phrase, the new Ohio citation system does *not* italicize Latin words. I have here for emphasis. But if you choose to use Latin terms do not italicize, at least in Ohio. In other states, check your system.

Rule 33
You May Split Infinitives— But Not Often

Usually, an infinitive—a verb phrase containing *to*—should not be split. That is, the *to* should immediately precede the verb: *to exit quickly* rather than *to quickly exit*. But you may freely split the infinitive if your ear tells you it is okay—or if the meaning is different.

What is the most famous split infinitive? *To boldly go where no one has gone before.* It would be weaker if we unsplit the infinitive: *To go boldly.* The former is stronger. Just use your ear. But if you are not sure of your ear, prefer the unsplit infinitive.

Rule 34
Commas and Periods Inside Quotes—Always

This was covered in Rule 28 as an aside. But quotation marks are wrong in so much legal and non-legal writing that this has graduated into a separate rule. Not a day goes by that I don't find mistakes in quotation marks.

In American English, all punctuation goes inside the quotation marks, with the exception of exclamation points, question marks, colons, and semicolons. This is true whether the quotation is a whole sentence or a fragment.

WRONG	RIGHT
Williams believes that "might makes right".	Williams believes that "might makes right."
Smith said, "I am not going", and stayed seated.	Smith said, "I am not going," and stayed seated.
The author wrote: "We cannot abide consistency".	The author wrote: "We cannot abide consistency."

In Commonwealth English, the opposite is true. So if you see a Canadian, British, Indian, or Australian quotation, the periods and commas follow the same rule as the one below for question marks and exclamation points.

But we are in America—you must get it right. An easy way to check, if you don't have this or Garner's book handy, is to simply look at a book printed in the United States. I have never seen a book get it wrong; but it's a whole diferent story with briefs, brochures, ads, and videos.

By their nature, colons and semicolons go outside the end of a quote, even if the original had a colon or a semicolon in that position.

WRONG	**RIGHT**
The court quotes Shakespeare: "To be or not to be;" it then overruled the objection.	The court quotes Shakespeare: "To be or not to be"; it then overruled the objection.

The only time you have to make a decision where punctuation goes is when you have a question mark or an exclamation point. These go inside the quote marks if they are part of the quotation, outside if they are not.

WRONG	RIGHT
Smith said, "Get Help"! and ran.	Smith said, "Get Help!" and ran.
The court said, "The Constitution does not apply in my courtroom!"	The court said, "The Constitution does not apply in my courtroom"! (assuming the emphasis is yours)
The judge asked: "Are you ready for trial"?	The judge asked: "Are you ready for trial?"

Notice above that short quotations may be introduced by either a colon or a comma. Prefer the colon when (1) it introduces something more formal or something said in a formal atmosphere, and (2) the source is identified before the colon. If you do not want to have to remember that suggestion (it is not a rule), then you will not be wrong if you always use a comma.

Sometimes the quote can simply be part of the sentence, usually preceded by that: We all know that "no good deed goes unpunished." This formulation requires no additional punctuation.

If you insist on using longer quotations—more than 50 words (Bluebook) or more than 100 (Painter)—they should be single-spaced and indented on both sides, without quotation marks. Quotation marks within the indented quote stay as they are. But see Rule 28—use long quotations sparingly. The longer the quote, the less chance the reader will read it. We do not use block quotes at all.

Rule 35
Remember the Reader

We touched on this in an earlier rule, but I have come to believe it is important enough to separate into a free-standing rule. Put yourself in the reader's place. Look through your reader's spectacles, not yours.

The problem is that you know all about your case or issue; and the reader generally knows nothing before reading your document. You know what you want to convey (we hope). The reader has no idea of your message unless you can convey it.

Even if you have followed all the rules, leave your work aside a day or two and read it through again. And have a non-lawyer read it to see if it makes sense.

Be sure to put your document through the readability calculations of your word-processing program. It will tell you the grade level, the percentage of passive-voice sentences, and the average sentence length (remember the 1818 Rule). These figures are not totally accurate, but they will give you a rough idea of the degree of difficulty the reader will encounter. If the document tests too high, revise it. Hint: the easiest way to improve the readability score is by shortening sentences. Improve your work by having periods run through it.

Rule 36
Learn the Styles Function of Word

Word is almost universal now. Whether it is better than Word Perfect is probably irrelevant, because it has so much of the marketplace. Lawyers were among the last holdouts for Word Perfect. But most of us have changed, because Word "came with" our computer. And clients use it.

The styles function allows you to set a "style" that includes (1) the font type, size, bolding or italics; (2) the spacing ("exactly" 26 point. for double space), and (3) the indents, tabs, and other spacing commands. Set different styles for your normal text, headings, and footnotes.

If you master the styles commands, you can change any part of your document without disturbing the rest. For example, if you want to change the text to single space rather than double, you just change the setting for normal—and the rest of your document (footnotes, headings, etc.) keeps its formatting.

Obviously, this takes much more explanation than I am able to offer here. But mostly it takes practice and experimentation. But once you (and your staff) master it, it will make changing documents around much easier. It is well worth the effort.

Rule 37
Use Lists to Simplify

Using lists can improve readability by ousting duplication. Consider the following paragraph:

Appellant sets forth three assignments of error. First, that the trial court erred in granting Appellee's motion for summary judgment with respect to the commercial automobile policy. Second, that the trial court erred in granting Appellee's motion for summary judgment with respect to the commercial general liability policy. Third, that the trial court erred in granting Appellee's motion for summary judgment with respect to the common-law claims.

See how much better it reads this way:

Smith contends that the trial court erred by granting summary judgment for State Mutual concerning (1) the commercial-automobile policy; (2) the commercial-general-liability policy; and (3) the common-law claims.

We have cut the number of words by more than half—31 versus 68. And we have gained, not lost, meaning.

Rule 38
Limit Subordinate Clauses

Too many clauses in one sentence may confuse the reader. Lawyers are especially fond of clauses beginning with *that*.

> Carter asserts *that* the fact *that* he was intoxicated cannot be used in a case *that* does not turn on the fact that the driver was intoxicated.

Rewritten:

> Carter asserts *that* his intoxication is irrelevant in this case.

The sentence now has one *that,* not four; 10 words, not 27. And its meaning is clearer. Also remember Rule 19—the above examples correctly use *that*, not *which*.

Or:

> Carter's intoxication is irrelevant.

Four words. Even better!

Rule 39
Use the Possessive Before Gerunds

A gerund is a verb converted to a noun by adding an -ing. Gerunds should not be confused with participles—verbs converted to adjectives by adding the *-ing*. The former take a possessive form of the preceding noun or pronoun; the latter do not.

The suspect's fleeing the scene was foolhardy. (*Fleeing* is a gerund—it requires a possessive.)

The suspect fleeing the scene was shot. (*Fleeing* here is an adjective describing suspect—no possessive.)

Personal pronouns especially require this construction.

I appreciate your helping me with the project.

My fondest memory of that trip was my meeting Sam.

The problem was his dozing at work.

But use your ear. Some words do not take the possessive, such as words that already end in *s*.

The members were upset at the thought of the ducks being killed.

Most often, though, the possessive should be used before the gerund. Put in the apostrophe, and sound out the sentence.

His taking the course was a good idea.

Smith's holding that office was temporary.

The professor was shocked by his making the grade.

This rule is not absolute, but good writers follow it. Sloppy writers do not.

Rule 40
Avoid the "Headnote" Style

Someone, somewhere, must have decreed that headnotes, or syllabi, had to be written in one sentence. That person should be drawn and quartered, at the very least. Why would anyone want to write long sentences, which necessarily need many clauses, to explain a court's holding? Read this one:

> Section 4943(B)(2)(c) of the Code, providing for the filing of a surety bond by all licensed dealers in securities, is not rendered unconstitutional by paragraph (d) thereof, allowing the commissioner of securities to determine the amount of the bond without providing any rule or condition by which the commissioner shall be governed in making such determination.

The last part of the sentence almost meets itself. Another example:

> When an employee engaged in the work of leveling a roadway is sent to his work by a superior, just prior to the inception of an electrical storm, equipped with a steel shovel, and while with the

steel shovel in his hands he is struck by lightning and killed, the steel shovel in the employee's hands subjects him to hazards greater than that of the general public in the community, and if such fact is proven by his dependent wife, she is entitled to participate in the state insurance fund.

The sentence reads that the electrical storm was equipped with a steel shovel. The readability is approximately zero. It could be rewritten as two sentences:

When an employee with a steel shovel is sent to work outside by a superior just before an electrical storm, the steel shovel in the employee's hands subjects him to hazards greater than that of the general community. If, holding the steel shovel, he is struck by lightning and killed, his spouse is entitled to participate in the state insurance fund.

The revision is now 61 words rather than 90, and it might be readable. You do not have to state your case in one sentence.

West's key numbers are another example. They are one sentence, no matter how long it has to be:

Trial court's improper refusal to allow manslaughter defendant to introduce particular treatises for impeachment purposes prevented jury from adequately assessing credibility of state's experts and prevented defendant from exercising full scope of his constitutional right to cross-examine witnesses, materially prejudicing defendant and requiring reversal, where experts testified that victim's death must have occurred immediately after a fatal blow to his head, and treatises sought to be introduced by defendant suggested that some victims of head injuries survived for up to three days after their injury.

The sentence is 84 words. Connectors like *where* and *and* string clauses together.

Convictions for intimidation and sham legal process were not based upon defendant's erroneous interpretation of the law that negated the "knowingly," "materially false," "fraudulent," "reckless," or "purported" requirement of such offenses; evidence was presented that defendant was aware of the existence of the fact that he was issuing documents not recognized as legal by state law, but which were titled in a manner or using such language to purport to be indictments or judgments or unilateral contracts that affected the public servants in their duties or required them to pay large sums of money to defendant if the public servant acted or failed to act as defendant wanted.

This one is 108 words. Note the *aware of the existence of the fact that*. How about just a*ware that*, or *knew*. There is no rule that syllabi, or headnotes, or case statements be in one sentence. Period.

The Message is the Message

Remember, the form is not everything, but it is very important. The medium is not the message; the message is the message. But if the message is not conveyed to the reader, it is not even a message.

Law is, after all, an art. It is not a science. There is science involved—word processing, Internet legal research, email. But the words in the processing come from us. Words are our parts inventory in the business of law. The collection of words into documents is our major product.

The turning of words into a product—a brief, a trust, an opinion letter—is not a job of easy assembly. It is art. And the more vivid our colors, the sharper our images, the more effective our art. The message is the message—but we must make it as clear and vibrant as we know how.

We Can Do Better

This book is only a start. I hope you have picked up a few points that [not *which*] will improve your writing.

Be sure to attend any legal writing seminars that are available. I have been to many, and always learn something. The best is Bryan Garner; even if you have to travel to hear him, it will be well worth the trip.

The books in the bibliography are my favorites, but there are, and will be, many others. Though I may disagree with a few points in some books, almost all agree on the basics—shorter sentences, shorter paragraphs, no lawspeak.

Some judges believe that we write only for lawyers. Lawyers sometimes think they write only for other lawyers and judges. But we should strive to be understandable to everyone. Laypeople will not necessarily be able to look up citations; but if we take citations out of the body of our documents, they might be able to read what we write. After all, the cases involve real people—shouldn't they be able to read what is happening to them?

We have talked mostly about form. Dressing your message in the best clothes will not make it eloquent; it will only make it presentable. But remember this:

> Law is not just a bunch of dusty old precepts to be applied with humdrum objectivity. It is alive; blood courses through its veins. As often as not, to apply legal rules you must weigh, judge, and argue about human folkways and human foibles. And to do that well, you must have a heart.[35]

To persuade a court, tell us why you should win—not just in dry legal terms, but in language that brings alive the human issues. "For in the end, the law has something to do with justice."[36]

Write well and do justice.

---

35. Garner, Elements of Legal Style, 174.
36. Id.

Bibliography

** Books you *must* have.
(*All in Ohio Citation Form*)

Books

Black's Law Dictionary (8th Ed. 2004)

Faulk & Miller, The Elements of Legal Writing (1994)

Garner's Modern American Usage (2003)

** Garner, A Dictionary of Modern Legal Usage (2nd Ed. 1995)

** Garner, The Elements of Legal Style (2nd Ed. 2002)

Garner, The Redbook – A Manual on Legal Style (2002)

** Garner, The Winning Brief: 100 Tips for Persuasive Briefing in Trial and Appellate Courts (2d Ed. 2004)

Shapiro, The Oxford Dictionary of American Legal Quotations (1993)

** Strunk & White, The Elements of Style (4th Ed. 1999)

** Tiersma, Legal Language (1999)

Williams, Style: Ten Lessons in Clarity and Grace (6th Ed. 1999)

Wydick, Plain English for Lawyers, (4th Ed. 1998)

Articles

Bramfield, Love Those Law Reviews, The Scribes Journal of Legal Writing (1994–1995), 101.

Butt, Plain Language in Property Law (1999), 73 Australian Law Journal, 807.

Kimble, Writing for Dollars, Writing to Please, The Scribes Journal of Legal Writing (1996–1997), 1

Kimble, Answering the Critics of Plain Language, The Scribes Journal of Legal Writing (1994–1995), 71

Mikva, Goodbye to Footnotes (1985), 56 U.Col.L. Rev. 647

Rodell, Goodbye to Law Reviews (1936), 23 Va.L. Rev. 38

Some Interesting Cases

Kohlbrand v. Ranieri, 159 Ohio App.3d 140, 2005-Ohio-295, 863 N.E.2d 76.

Dunkelman v. Cincinnati Bengals, Inc., 158 Ohio App.3d 604, 2004-Ohio-6425, 820 N.E.2d 926.

Gibson v. Donahue, 148 Ohio App.3d, 2002-Ohio-165, 772 N.E.2d 646.

State v. Bowen (2000), 139 Ohio App.3d 41, 742 N.E.2d 1166.

Klein v. Leis, 146 Ohio App.3d 526, 2002-Ohio-1634, 767 N.E.2d 286.

Cincinnati ex rel. Ritter v. Cincinnati Reds, L.L.C., 150 Ohio App.3d 778, 2002-Ohio-7078, 782 N.E.2d 1225.

Cincinnati Entertainment Assoc. v. Bd. of Commrs. (2001), 141 Ohio App.3d 803, 753 N.E.2d 884.

Vermeer of S. Ohio, Inc. v. Argo Constr. Co. (2001), 144 Ohio App.3d 271, 760 N.E.2d 1.

Biography

JUDGE MARK P. PAINTER was elected to the Ohio First District Court of Appeals in 1994 and re-elected without opposition in 2000. For the previous 13 years, Judge Painter served on the Hamilton County Municipal Court.

A Cincinnati native, Judge Painter attended the University of Cincinnati, where he was elected Student Body President in 1969, receiving a B.A. in 1970, and a J.D. in 1973. He practiced law for nine years before becoming a judge, mainly with a firm that later became part of Thompson Hine.

Judge Painter is recognized as one of the outstanding legal scholars in Ohio. As a municipal court judge, he was the most-published trial judge in the state. More than 300 of Judge Painter's decisions have been published national-ly, making him one of the most-published judges in Ohio history.

In adddition to this book, now in its third edition, he is the author of *Ohio Driving Under the Influence Law* (WestGroup, now in its 14th edition), the only legal textbook on DUI in Ohio. He is coauthor of *Ohio Appellate Practice* (WestGroup). Judge Painter has also authored 91 articles for legal journals. He has written a biography, *William Howard Taft: President & Chief Justice* (Jarndyce & Jarndyce Press, 2004). He is currently working on a biography of Warren G. Harding.

As an Adjunct Professor at the University of Cincinnati College of Law since 1990, Judge Painter taught Agency and Partnership for 12 years, and now teaches advanced legal writing. He teaches DUI law, appellate practice, legal writing, and legal ethics to judges and lawyers throughout the country. He has lectured at more than 140 seminars across the country for, among others, the Ohio Judicial College, the National Institute of Trial Advocacy, Professional Education Systems Institute, and the Ohio State Bar Association C.L.E. Institute.

Judge Painter has served as a Trustee of the Cincinnati Freestore/Foodbank, the Cincinnati Bar Association, the Friends of the William Howard Taft Birthplace, and the Citizens School Committee. He is a Master of the Bench

Emeritus of the Potter Stewart Inn of Court, and served for three years as a member of the Ohio Supreme Court Board of Commissioners on Grievances and Discipline.

Judge Painter is a member of the Cincinnati, Ohio State, and American Bar Associations, the American Society of Writers on Legal Subjects (Scribes), the Plain Language International Network, the Legal Writing Institute, Clarity, and the American Judicature Society.

Mark and his wife, Sue Ann Painter, were married in 1986. They live in the Cincinnati neighborhood of Clifton Heights-Fairview.

Judge Painter is happy to do legal-writing seminars for firms, corporations, or bar associations anywhere in the country. For information, please contact him through the website below.

www.judgepainter.org

ADDENDUM
STATE CITATION / BRIEF REQUIREMENTS
CONTACT INFORMATION

In this edition of *The Legal Writer*, we have provided additional information related to individual state citation and brief style requirements. In addition, we have provided internet links to the states' court systems as well as addresses and phone numbers of the clerks of the supreme court (or equivalent).

Although we feel that the citation style requirements reflect the reporting methods preferred by the individual states' supreme court at the time of publication, we strongly suggest that you contact the clerk of court in the jurisdiction where the case is being heard; the "uniform" style requirements can change and may vary from jurisdiction to jurisdiction within a state.

The Association of Reporters of Judicial Decisions is a good resource for locating contact information for clerks from numerous jurisdictions. The website address for the ARJD is:
http://arjd.washlaw.edu

ALABAMA
http://www.judicial.state.al.us

Citations: Alabama recognizes both of the following rules of style to apply to citations and briefs:

The *Harvard Bluebook: A Uniform System of Citation* or

ALWD Citation Manual: A Professional System of Citation

Further information regarding reporting styles can be found in Alabama's *Rules of Appellate Procedure: Rule 28-BRIEFS.*

Alabama Contact Information:
Reporter of Decisions
Alabama Supreme Court
300 Dexter Ave.
Montgomery, AL 36104-3741
Telephone: 334-242-4621
Fax: 334-242-4483

ALASKA
http://www.state.ak.us/courts

Briefs: *Alaska Rules of Appellate Procedure Part II. Procedure on Appeals as of Right—Rule 212.*
http://www.state.ak.us/courts/app.htm#212

Citations: Alaska subscribes to the *Harvard Bluebook* style of citation. General information can be found at:

Alaska Contact Information:
Clerk-Supreme Court of Alaska
303 K Street
Anchorage, Alaska 99501
Telephone: 907-264-0608
Fax: 907-264-0878

ARIZONA
http://www.supreme.state.az.us

Briefs: Arizona Rules of Civil Appellate Procedure (*ARCAP*), *Rules 13-15*.
http://azrules.westgroup.com/home/azrules/default.wl

Arizona Contact Information:
Clerk of the Court
1501 W. Washington, Suite 402
Phoenix, AZ 85007-3231
Telephone: 602-542-9396

ARKANSAS
http://courts.state.ar.us

Citations: Arkansas uses its own *House Style Guide* which applies generally to all aspects of citation and court reporting. The Arkansas *House Style Guide* can be downloaded at:
http://courts.state.ar.us/courts/rd_style.html

Arkansas Contact Information:
Reporter of Decisions
Justice Building
625 Marshall Street
Little Rock, AR 72201
Telephone: 501-682-9400
Fax: 501-682-6877

CALIFORNIA
http://www.courtinfo.ca.gov

Briefs: The information for California style for briefs can be found at:
http://www.courtinfo.ca.gov/rules/titleone/title1-2-28.htm

Citations: The *California Style Manual* is the handbook of legal style for California courts and lawyers. It was written by the Reporter of Decisions of the California State Supreme Court and is issued under approval of the State Supreme Court. The latest edition is for sale at:
http://west.thomson.com/product/12231786/product.asp

California Contact Information:
  Reporter of Decisions
  Supreme Court of California
  350 McAllister Street
  San Francisco, CA 94102-3600
Telephone: 415-865-7160
Fax: 415-865-7159

COLORADO
http://www.coloradosupremecourt.com

Citations: The legal citation format can be found in the Colorado Revised Statute *§2-5-101(3) C.R.S.* A link to the Colorado State Statutes can be found at:

http://www.courts.state.co.us/siteindex.htm
Click on *Colorado State Statutes* which will take you to the LexisNexis website.

Colorado Contact Information:
  Reporter of Decisions
  Colorado State Judicial Building
  2 East 14th Ave., Fourth Floor
  Denver, CO 80220
Telephone: 303-837-3738
Fax: 303-837-3702

CONNECTICUT
http://www.jud.state.ct.us

Citations: Connecticut has produced its own citation style manual entitled: *Manual of Style for Connecticut Courts*. It is available from:

  Connecticut Commission on Legal Publications
  111 Phoenix Avenue
  Enfield, CT 06082
  Order Telephone: 860-741-3027

Connecticut Contact Information:
Reporter of Judicial Decisions
Supreme Court of Connecticut
Drawer N, Station "A"
Hartford, Connecticut 06106
Telephone: 860-757-2250
Fax: 860-757-2213

DELAWARE
http://courts.state.de.us

Citations: For Reported Opinions, the Delaware Supreme Court recognizes the *Harvard Bluebook* as its source for citation reporting.

For Unreported Opinions, it recognizes either the *LEXIS Citation Form, Westlaw Citation Form* or the *Delaware Citation Form*. See the Delaware Supreme Court rules located at:
http://courts.state.de.us/Rules/?supremerules.pdf
Rule 14(g) *Uniform System of Citation (Harvard Bluebook)*
Rule 93(c) *Citations*

Delaware Contact Information:
Court Administrator-Supreme Court of Delaware
55 The Green
Supreme Court Building
Dover, DE 19903
Telephone: 302-577-3706

DISTRICT OF COLUMBIA
http://www.dcappeals.gov (*Court of Appeals website*)

Briefs: The information for District of Columbia style for briefs can be found in Rule 32 of the Rules for the Court of Appeals located at:
http://www.dcappeals.gov/dccourts/appeals/rules.jsp

Citations: The District of Columbia uses an addendum to *Harvard Bluebook* entitled the *Citation Guidance Memorandum* which can be found at:
http://www.dccourts.gov/dccourts/docs/Revised_Citation_Guide.pdf

District of Columbia Contact Information:
Clerk-Court of Appeals
Room 6000
500 Indiana Avenue, N.W.
Washington, DC 20001
Telephone: 202-879-2725

FLORIDA
http://www.floridasupremecourt.org

Citations: The Florida Uniform Citation System can be found under *Florida Rules of Procedure,* Rule 9.800.

The Florida Supreme Court generally recognizes the *Harvard Bluebook* as the source for its citation style guidelines. However, it also utilizes the *Florida Style Manual* published by the Florida State University Law Review. A copy of the *Florida Style Manual* can be downloaded at:
http://www.law.fsu.edu/journals/lawreview/downloads/242/fsm.pdf

Florida Contact Information:
Reporter of Decisions, Florida Supreme Court
500 South Duval Street
Tallahassee FL 32399-1925
Telephone: 850-922-9793
Fax: 850-487-4696

GEORGIA
http://www.gasupreme.us

Citations: Although the Georgia Supreme Court is not officially on record as adopting a specific citation style, it accepts a style that approximates the *Harvard Bluebook.*

Georgia Contact Information:
Reporter of Decisions, Supreme Court of Georgia
244 Washington Street, S.W.
Suite 423
Atlanta, Georgia 30334
Telephone: 404-656-3470
Fax: 404-651-2253

HAWAII
http://www.courts.state.hi.us

Briefs: http://www.courts.state.hi.us/index.jsp
Click **RULES**—find **APPELLATE Rule 28.**

Citations: Hawaii rules do not require a particular citation style. *HRAP 28(b)(1)* merely requires that Hawaii cases be cited to both the state and regional reporter, foreign cases need only be cited to the regional reporter.

Hawaii Contact Information:
Clerk of Courts
P.O. Box 2560
Honolulu, Hawaii 96804
Telephone: 808-539-4732
Fax: 808-539-4928

IDAHO
http://www.isc.idaho.gov

Citations: Rule 15 of Idaho's Internal Rules of the Idaho Supreme Court specifies the *Harvard Bluebook.*
> *"Citations appearing in opinions shall be in conformity with statutory provision of this state, the rules of this Court and if not therein covered, in conformity with the current edition of A Uniform System of Citation, published and distributed by the Harvard Law Review Association."*

See: **http://www.isc.idaho.gov/rules/internal.pdf**

Idaho Contact Information:
Reporter and Clerk of Courts
Supreme Court of Idaho
451 West State Street
Boise, ID 83720
Telephone: 208-334-2210

ILLINOIS
http://www.state.il.us/court

Briefs: Illinois Supreme Court Rule 341(d)
http://www.state.il.us/court/SupremeCourt/Rules/Art_III

Citations: Illinois Supreme Court Rule 6
http://www.state.il.us/court/SupremeCourt/Rules/Art_I

Illinois Contact Information:
Reporter of Decisions
Illinois Supreme Court
P.O. Box 3456
Bloomington, IL 61702
Telephone: 309-827-8513
Fax: 309-828-4651

INDIANA
http://www.in.gov/judiciary/supreme

Citations: The Indiana Supreme Court considers the *Harvard Bluebook* as:
"[t]he best general source of information concerning the proper form of a citation to legal authority..."

http://www.in.gov/judiciary/center/pubs/benchbooks/court-reporter
Go to Appendix C.

Indiana Contact Information:
Clerk of the Supreme Court
200 West Washington Street
217 State House
Indianapolis, IN 46204

Telephone: 317-232-1930
Fax: 317-232-8365

IOWA
http://www.judicial.state.ia.us

Briefs: http://www.legis.state.ia.us/Rules/Current/court/gna1.pdf
Court Rules—Iowa Rules of Appellate Procedure 6.14-6.17

Citations: Iowa uses the *Harvard Bluebook* as its citation system guide.

Iowa Contact Information:
Clerk of the Iowa Supreme Court
State House
Des Moines, IA 50319
Telephone: 515-281-5911
Fax: 515-242-6164

KANSAS
http://www.kscourts.org

Citations:
Kansas uses a hybrid version of the *Harvard Bluebook* and the *Chicago Maroon Book*. There is also a citation pamphlet that is distributed to judges and the staff of the appellate courts, but it is not available to the general public.

Kansas Contact Information:
Reporter of Decisions
Kansas Judicial Center
301 West 10th
Topeka, KS 66612-1598
Telephone: 785-296-3214
Fax: 785-296-7076

KENTUCKY
http://www.kycourts.net

Briefs: Section 76.12 of the Kentucky Rules of Civil Procedure that addresses filing of briefs can be found at:
http://kyrules.west.thomson.com/home/kyrules/default.wl
Go to: *Rules of Civil Procedure—Appeals—Rule 76.12*

Citations: Kentucky *Rules of Civil Procedure 76.12(4)(g) Form of Citations.*
"All citations of Kentucky Statutes shall be made from the official edition of the Kentucky Revised Statutes and may be abbreviated 'KRS.'"

Kentucky Contact Information:
Supreme Court Administrator / General Council
Capitol building, Room 235
Frankfort, KY 40601
Telephone: 502-564-4176
Fax: 502-564-2665

LOUISIANA
http://www.lasc.org

Citations: Louisiana Supreme Court Rules *Section 8. Citation of Louisiana Appellate Decisions.*
http://www.lasc.org/rules/html/g8.html

Louisiana Contact Information:
Clerk of Court
Supreme Court of Louisiana
400 Royal Street, Suite 4200
New Orleans, LA 70130-8102
Telephone: 504-310-2300

MAINE
http://www.courts.state.me.us

Citations: The *Uniform Maine Citations*, published by the Maine Law Review, is used when citing Maine court opinions. The *Harvard Bluebook* is also used. However in cases of a dispute, the *Uniform Maine Citations* guidebook takes precedence as described in Chapter 5—Section 3 of the *Maine Legislative Drafting Manual.*
http://janus.state.me.us/legis/ros/manual/Webdman-16.htm

Maine Contact Information:
Clerk of Court and Reporter of Decisions
Maine Supreme Judicial Court
142 Federal Street
P.O. Box 368
Portland, ME 04112
Telephone: 207-822-4146

MARYLAND
http://www.courts.state.md.us

Briefs: Style of briefs is described in Maryland Court Rule 8-503—Style and Form of Briefs which can be found at:
http://198.187.128.12/maryland/lpext.dll?f=templates&fn=fs-main.htm&2.0

Citations: Maryland uses the *Harvard Bluebook* as its guide for citation style.

Maryland Contact Information:
Clerk of Court of Appeals and Reporter of Decisions
Court of Appeals of Maryland
361 Rowe Blvd.
Annapolis, MD 21401
Telephone: 410-269-3539

MASSACHUSETTS
http://www.mass.gov/courts

Citations: Massachusetts has produced its own *Supreme Judicial Court Official Reports Style Manual* which can be found at:
www.massreports.com/sjcstyle04.pdf

Massachusetts Contact Information:
Reporter of Decisions
Supreme Judicial Court of Massachusetts
1407 New Court House
Boston, MA 02108
Telephone: 617-557-1196
Fax: 617-557-1105

MICHIGAN
http://www.courts.michigan.gov

Citations: Administrative Order No.1987-2 requires that legal citations be issued using the format delineated by the *Michigan Style Manual*. This rule can be found at:
http://courtofappeals.mijud.net/rules/public/default.asp
Go to: *Michigan Uniform System of Citation* to find Admin. Order No.1987-2.

Michigan Contact Information:
    Reporter of Decisions, Supreme Court of Michigan
    Michigan Hall of Justice
    P.O. Box 30052
    Lansing, MI 48909
Telephone: 517-373-5243
Fax: 517-373-8989

MINNESOTA
http://www.courts.state.mn.us

Citations: Minnesota uses the *Harvard Bluebook* style of citation reporting.

Minnesota Contact Information:
    Opinion Clerk, Minnesota Supreme Court
    25 Constitution Avenue
    305 Minnesota Judicial Center
    St. Paul, MN 55155
Telephone: 612-296-8579

MISSISSIPPI
http://www.mssc.state.ms.us/

Citations: Mississippi has no specific rule that denotes their style guidelines, but has a long-standing practice of accepting the *Harvard Bluebook* style of citation reporting.

Mississippi Contact Information:
    Clerk of the Supreme Court
    Supreme Court of Mississippi
    P.O. Box 249
    Jackson, MS 39205
Telephone: 601-359-3697
Fax: 601-359-2407

MISSOURI
http://www.courts.mo.gov

Citations: Missouri has no prescribed guidelines for citations.

Missouri Contact Information:
Deputy Clerk, Court en Blanc
Missouri Supreme Court
P.O. Box 150
Jefferson City, MO 65102

Telephone: 573-751-7313
Fax: 573-751-2809

MONTANA
http://www.lawlibrary.state.mt.us/

Briefs: Montana's *Rule 23 Briefs of the Appellate Procedure* can be found at:
http://data.opi.state.mt.us/bills/mca_toc/25_21_V.htm

Citations: Go to:
http://montanabar.org/montanalawyer/september2002/citation.

Montana Contact Information:
State Reporter of the Montana Supreme Court
P.O. Box 749
Helena, MT 59624
Telephone: 406-449-8889
Fax: 406-449-4083

NEBRASKA
http://court.nol.org/courts.htm

Briefs: Supreme Court Rules of Practice and Procedure 9 C(4). *General Rules for Preparation of Briefs* states:
> *"Nebraska cases shall be cited by the Nebraska Reports and/or Nebraska Appellate Reports, but may include citation to such other reports as may contain such cases."*

http://court.nol.org/rules/pracproc.htm

Nebraska Contact Information:
Reporter of Decisions, Nebraska Supreme Court
Room 1214, State Capitol
Lincoln, NE 68509-8910
Telephone: 402-471-3010
Fax: 402-471-2197

NEVADA
http://www.nvsupremecourt.us

Briefs: Nevada guidelines for briefs can be found at:
http://leg.state.nv.us/CourtRules/NRAP.html

Citations: Nevada uses the *Harvard Bluebook* style of citation reporting with some slight variations as prescribed in *Law Clerk Handbook.*

Nevada Contact Information:
Clerk of Court, Nevada Supreme Court
201 South Carson Street
Carson City, NV 89701-4702

Telephone: 775-684-1600
Fax: 775-684-1601

NEW HAMPSHIRE
http://www.courts.state.nh.us

Briefs: Rules for Briefs are located at:
http://www.courts.state.nh.us/rules/scr/scr-16.htm

New Hampshire Contact Information:
Reporter of Decisions, Supreme Court of New Hampshire
Noble Drive
Concord, NH 03301
Telephone: 603-271-2646
Fax: 603-271-6630

NEW JERSEY
http://www.judiciary.state.nj.us

Citations: New Jersey's Style Manual can be found at:
http://www.judiciary.state.nj.us/appdiv/manualofstyle.pdf

New Jersey Contact Information:
Clerk of the Supreme Court of New Jersey
Box CN970
Trenton, NJ 08625
Telephone: 609-292-4837

NEW MEXICO
www.supremecourt.nm.org

Citations: New Mexico's citation rule is *23-112 NMRA*, which may be accessed from the court's website by clicking on *New Mexico Statute and Court Rules;* then typing *23-112 NMRA* into the *Search* box.

New Mexico Contact Information:
Chief Clerk of the Supreme Court of New Mexico
P.O. Box 848
Santa Fe, NM 87504
Telephone: 505-827-4860
Fax: 505-827-4837

NEW YORK
http://www.courts.state.ny.us

Citations: New York has produced its own citation guidebook entitled, *The New York Law Reports Style Manual.* It can be found at:
http://www.courts.state.ny.us/reporter/New_Styman.htm

New York Contact Information:
State Reporter, New York State Law Reporting Bureau
One Commerce Plaza, Suite 1750
Albany, NY 12210
Telephone: 518-474-8211
Fax: 518-463-6869

NORTH CAROLINA
http://www.nccourts.org

Citations: North Carolina has developed its own citation system as found in *A Style Manual for the North Carolina Rules of Appellate Procedure.* Go to:
http://www.aoc.state.nc.us/www/public/html/pdf/stylemanual.pdf

North Carolina Contact Information:
Appellate Division Reporter
Supreme Court of North Carolina
P.O. Box 2170
Raleigh, NC 23501
Telephone: 919-733-3710

NORTH DAKOTA
http://www.court.state.nd.us/

Briefs: All briefs must conform to the style required by *N.D.R.App.P. RULE 28. BRIEFS* and can be found at:
http://www.ndcourts.com/rules/appellat/frameset.htm

Citations: North Dakota has developed its own citation style guide. See:
http://www.ndcourts.com/citation/

North Dakota Contact Information:
Clerk of the Supreme Court of North Dakota
State Capitol, 1st Floor
Bismark, ND 58505-0530
Telephone: 701-382-2221

OHIO
http://www.sconet.state.oh.us

Citations: The *Ohio Manual of the Forms of Citations Used in the Ohio Official Reports* appears in Volume 88 Ohio App.3d. can be found on the Supreme Court's website at:
http://www.sconet.state.oh.us/ROD/pdf/mancite.pdf

Ohio Contact Information:
Supreme Court of Ohio Reporter's Office
30 E. Broad St., Second Floor
Columbus, Ohio 43266
Telephone: 614-466-4961
Fax: 614-752-4418

OKLAHOMA
http://www.oscn.net

Citations: Oklahoma Supreme Court Rule-*1.200* in *Section VII* delineates the Official Paragraph Form for citation styles. It is located at:
http://www.oscn.net/applications/oscn/deliverdocument.asp?citeID=73621

Oklahoma Contact Information:
Clerk of the Supreme Court of Oklahoma
State Capitol, Room 1
Oklahoma City, OK 73105
Telephone: 405-521-2163

OREGON
http://www.ojd.state.or.us

Citations: Oregon has adopted its own *Appellate Court Style Manual* which can be found at:
http://www.publications.ojd.state.or.us/
Click on *Style Manual.*

Oregon Contact Information:
Editor-Composer, Oregon Appellate Courts
Supreme Court Building
1163 State Street
Salem, OR 97310-0260
Telephone: 503-986-5567
Fax: 503-986-5934

PENNSYLVANIA
http://www.courts.state.pa.us

Briefs: Requirements for filing a brief can be found at:
http://www.courts.state.pa.us/Index/Supreme/briefguide.pdf

Citations: Pennsylvania uses the *Harvard Bluebook* style of citation reporting.

Pennsylvania Contact Information:
Reporter of Decisions
Supreme Court of Pennsylvania
601 South Office Building
Harrisburg, PA 17110
Telephone: 717-787-5065
Fax: 717-787-7427

RHODE ISLAND
http://www.courts.state.ri.us

Briefs: Guidelines for filing briefs can be found in the *Supreme Court Rules of Appellate Procedure Article 1 Rule 16.*

Rhode Island Contact Information:
Clerk of the Supreme Court of Rhode Island
250 Benefit Street
Providence, RI 02903
Telephone: 401-222-3272
Fax: 401-222-3599

SOUTH CAROLINA
http://www.judicial.state.sc.us

Citations: South Carolina *Section C, Rule 239 Citation of South Carolina Authority* addresses its preferred citation style. At the above website, click on *Court Rules;* go to *Rule 239.*

South Carolina Contact Information:
Supreme Court Reporter
Supreme Court of South Carolina
P.O. Box 11330
Columbia, SC 29211
Telephone: 803-734-1080

SOUTH DAKOTA
http://www.sdjudicial.com

Citations: South Dakota uses the *Harvard Bluebook* style of citation reporting.

South Dakota Contact Information:
Clerk of Court
Supreme Court of South Dakota
500 East Capitol Avenue
Pierre, SD 57501-5770
Telephone: 605-773-3511

TENNESSEE
http://www.tsc.state.tn.us

Briefs: Tennessee Court Rules *Section G* addresses the requirements for briefs. This information is located on the website above. Click on *Court Rules; Current Rules; Rules of Appellate Procedure;* go to *Section G.*

Tennessee Contact Information:
Administrative Office of the Courts
511 Union Street
Suite 600
Nashville, TN 37219
Telephone: 615-741-2687

TEXAS
http://www.supreme.courts.state.tx.us

Citations: Texas uses its own citation manual entitled, *Texas Rules of Form* and often referred to as the *Greenbook.* Order information can be found at UT Law Publications
E-mail : Publications@mail.law.utexas.edu
Telephone : 512-232-1149
Fax : 512-471-6988

Texas Contact Information:
Clerk of the Supreme Court of Texas
P.O. Box 12248
Austin, TX 78711
Telephone: 512-463-1312

UTAH
http://www.utcourts.gov

Citations: The *Utah Supreme Court Standing Order #4* addresses its citation requirements. This can be found at:
http://www.utcourts.gov/resources/rules/urap/Supctso.htm#4

Utah Contact Information:
Clerk of Court
Supreme Court of Utah
332 State Capitol
Salt Lake City, UT 84114
Telephone: 801-538-1044

VERMONT
http://www.vermontjudiciary.org

Citations: Vermont Court *Rule 28.2* defines citation expectations. Go to:
http://www.vermontjudiciary.org/rules/default.htm
This will take you to LexisNexis. Go to *Court Rules; Rules of Appellate Procedure; General Provisions; Rule 28.*

Vermont Contact Information:
Reporter of Decisions
Vermont Supreme Court
109 State Street
Montpelier, VT 05609-0801
Telephone: 802-828-4570
Fax: 802-828-4750

VIRGINIA
http://www.courts.state.va.us

Briefs: Briefs are addressed in the Virginia Court Rule *vscr-5A:4*.

Virginia Contact Information:
Clerk of the Supreme Court of Virginia
P.O. Box 5104
Charlottesville, VA 22905
Telephone: 804-786-6455
Fax: 804-786-4542

WASHINGTON STATE
http://www.courts.wa.gov

Citations: Washington State's citation guidelines can be found in GR 14 of its court rules. Go to:
http://www.courts.wa.gov/court_rules/
Click on *Court Rules* go to the *Search* box and type in *GR 14*.

Washington State Contact Information:
Reporter of Decisions
Supreme Court of Washington
Temple of Justice, P.O. Box 40920
Olympia, WA 98504-0929
Telephone: 360-357-2090
Fax: 360-357-2099

WEST VIRGINIA
http://www.state.wv.us/wvsca

Citations: West Virginia uses the *Harvard Bluebook* style of citation reporting.

West Virginia Contact Information:
Clerk of Courts
West Virginia Supreme Court of Appeals
State Capitol, Room 26E
Charleston, WV 25305
Telephone: 304-558-2601
Fax: 304-558-3815

WISCONSIN
http://www.courts.state.wi.us

Citations: Supreme Court Rule *SCR 80.02 Proper citation* delineates the requirements for citations in the state of Wisconsin.

Wisconsin Contact Information:
Clerk of the Wisconsin Supreme Court
110 East Main Street, Suite 215
P.O. Box 1688
Madison, WI 53701-1688
Telephone: 608-266-1880
Fax: 608-267-0640

WYOMING
http://courts.state.wy.us

Citations:
Wyoming subscribes to the *Harvard Bluebook* style of citation reporting.

Wyoming Contact Information:
Clerk of the Supreme Court of Wyoming
Supreme Court Building
Cheyenne, Wyoming 82002
Telephone: 307-777-7316
Fax: 307-777-6129

For Additional Copies of

THE LEGAL WRITER

Use the form below

JARNDYCE & JARNDYCE PRESS
DIVISION OF PSA CONSULTING, INC.
2449 FAIRVIEW AVENUE
CINCINNATI, OH 45219

PLEASE SEND ME _____ COPIES OF **THE LEGAL WRITER.**

MY CHECK FOR _____ IS ENCLOSED.

1-9 COPIES $26.95 + 1.89 TAX + 3.16 S&H = $32.00 EA.

10-50 COPIES $22.95 + 1.61 TAX + 2.44 S&H =$27.00 EA.

51-100 COPIES $18.95 + 1.33 TAX + 1.72 S&H =$22.00 EA.

100+ CALL TONY BRUNSMAN, 513-382-4315

NAME

ADDRESS

CITY   STATE   ZIP

PHONE   EMAIL